This little book is dedicated to my stat students:
Past, present, and future.

bare-bones R

A BRIEF INTRODUCTORY GUIDE

THOMAS P. HOGAN

University of Scranton

$SAGE

Los Angeles | London | New Delhi
Singapore | Washington DC

For information:

SAGE Publications, Inc.
2455 Teller Road
Thousand Oaks, California 91320
E-mail: order@sagepub.com

SAGE Publications Ltd.
1 Oliver's Yard
55 City Road
London EC1Y 1SP
United Kingdom

SAGE Publications India Pvt. Ltd.
B 1/I 1 Mohan Cooperative Industrial Area
Mathura Road, New Delhi 110 044
India

SAGE Publications Asia-Pacific Pte. Ltd.
33 Pekin Street #02-01
Far East Square
Singapore 048763

Printed in the United States of America

Library of Congress Cataloging-in-Publication Data

Hogan, Thomas P.
Bare-bones R: a brief introductory guide / Thomas P. Hogan.
    p. cm.
Includes bibliographical references and index.
ISBN 978-1-4129-8041-8 (pbk.)
    1. Social sciences—Statistical methods—Data processing. 2. Statistics—Data processing. 3. R (Computer program language) I. Title.

HA32.H64 2011
005.26′2—dc22   2009033530

This book is printed on acid-free paper.

09   10   11   12   13   10   9   8   7   6   5   4   3   2   1

Acquisitions Editor:	Vicki Knight
Associate Editor:	Lauren Habib
Editorial Assistant:	Ashley Dodd
Production Editor:	Carla Freeman
Copy Editor:	QuADS Prepress (P) Ltd.
Typesetter:	C&M Digitals (P) Ltd.
Proofreader:	Christina West
Cover Designer:	Stephanie Adams
Marketing Manager:	Gail Buschman

Contents

Preface

I intend this bare-bones introduction to R as a supplement to a standard first-course textbook in statistics or for those who have already completed such a course and now need to do some statistical analysis on their own. This introduction, as suggested by its title, is bare-bones. It doesn't pretend to teach everything about R—just to get people started with it.

R is a wonderful tool for statistical work. Its flexibility and richness offer a boon to experienced researchers. It also offers great advantages for statistical novices—those taking their first course in statistics. However, for such novices, R can be intimidating, precisely because of its flexibility and richness. Its arcane customs, symbols, and terminology may make the novice shudder. Some of the purported "introductions to R" seem like trying to teach Mozart concertos in the first week of piano lessons. They are just overwhelming. In my experience, extant introductions share the following drawbacks, not for the experienced researcher but for the novice. They tend to present several ways of accomplishing any given task (thus nicely illustrating R's richness), whereas the novice needs just one way to do it. They tend to use traditional R terminology (arguments of functions, vectors, etc.) rather than plain English. They are very short on examples. This feature helps their compactness, but novices need examples. They tend to include advanced statistical techniques (logistic regression, mixed-effects ANOVA, etc.), while the novice is still trying to learn the difference between a mean and a median. I have tried to avoid these drawbacks.

I make the following assumptions about the students using this bare-bones introduction:

- I assume that they are taking a first course in statistics or have already completed such a course. I'm not trying to teach statistical concepts and techniques such as mean, standard deviation, correlation coefficient, *t* test, and analysis of variance. I assume that the statistics instructor and textbook will cover these topics.
- I assume that they have experience with personal computers, the Internet, and a word processing system.
- I assume that they (and their instructors) can devote a very limited amount of time to this bare-bones introduction. I'd like to think one could get through this entire introduction, including working through the examples, in a few hours.
- I do *not* assume that they have had any prior experience in computer programming.
- Finally, I'm going to use the Windows platform. It's the most commonly available. R will work on other platforms, and much of what we cover here will work perfectly well on other platforms, but to keep things simple, I'm just using Windows.

Here are the guidelines I used in putting this material together:

- Start from the very beginning with each topic. This includes downloading R, R Commander, and an add-on package.
- Keep it short. Don't try to cover everything—just get started.
- Always include at least one example for anything that gets introduced.
- When there are several different ways to accomplish something, just present one, and move on.
- When it's necessary to introduce some of R's weird terms, try to give a translation into plain English or, at least, into the common language of elementary statistics.
- Use examples from the behavioral/social sciences. A lot of what we cover will work equally well in other fields, for example, biology, allied health fields, and business, but I've not tried to include examples from these other fields.
- Don't introduce any statistical techniques beyond those covered in the typical first course in statistics in the behavioral/social sciences. In fact,

don't even try to cover all the techniques in the first course. A sampling of them will do.

- Use textboxes, highlighting, varying fonts, and so on to enhance students' comprehension.
- Introduce both base R (and its usual add-on packages) and R Commander. As tempting as it is, I don't think doing R Commander by itself (or even first) is a good idea.

Occasionally, I must admit, I violate one of these rules—but only occasionally.

I realize that my assumptions and rules, as just outlined, may encourage my colleagues to pummel me with criticisms. Why introduce only this way to accomplish some task? What about this nifty add-on package? Won't this common English translation of a technical R term possibly mislead? And so on. I'll accept those criticisms. But I'll add a bet. If, within a few hours of instruction, I can get students feeling comfortable and confident using R, I'll bet those students will go on to learn a whole lot more about R on their own. We just need a good start.

In this book, Chapter 1 is a bare-bones introduction to base R and its usual add-on packages. Chapter 2 is a bare-bones introduction to R Commander. Chapter 3 covers frequently asked questions about just a few other topics that go barely beyond the bare-bones topics in Chapters 1 and 2. Skipping sections within Chapter 3, or even all of it, will not jeopardize the integrity of Chapters 1 and 2.

"Self-Checks" are scattered throughout to help the reader practice newly introduced procedures. Some readers may wish to skip these as the main text also includes practical examples of the procedures. Other readers will find that the Self-Checks help reinforce learning.

The book has a companion Web site, http://www.sagepub.com/BareBonesR, which contains downloadable data sets used in the text as well as selected updates for R and corrections to the text.

ACKNOWLEDGMENTS

It's amazing how many people deserve thanks even for a little book such as this one. Most obviously, thanks go to the R Development Core Team for continued maintenance, refinement, and expansion of the whole R project and to John Fox for development of R Commander. Section 3–6 of this book contains formal citations to their work. Special thanks to the reviewers of a draft of the manuscript for some very helpful suggestions:

David Atkins
University of Washington

Stephen Jessee
University of Texas at Austin

David C. Kimball
University of Missouri, St. Louis

Maureen Lahiff
University of California, Berkeley

Christopher C. Weiss
Columbia University

Toshiyuki Yuasa
University of Houston

A round of applause for four of my students (Ajeem Evans, Michael Frechen, Noel McFadden, and Eva Piatek) who volunteered to take time out from their graduation week festivities(!) to work through a penultimate draft and helped correct some crucial details and to Ms. Donna Rupp, our department's administrative assistant, who did the same, as well as serving as technical consultant on myriad fine points. Finally, thanks to Vicki Knight, Senior Acquisitions Editor at Sage Publications, for her enthusiasm and experience in shepherding the project along. You'd think with all that help, the book would be error-free. Alas, that's not likely, and I'll take the blame for that.

About the Author

Thomas P. Hogan, PhD, is Professor of Psychology and Distinguished University Fellow at the University of Scranton. He teaches courses in statistics, research methods, psychological testing, and educational assessment. He has received all three of the University's teaching awards. Prior to his time as full-time professor, he served as Dean of the Graduate School and Director of Research and as Interim Provost/Academic Vice President at Scranton. Previously, he was Professor of Psychology, Associate Chancellor for Graduate and Professional Programs, and Codirector of the Assessment Center at the University of Wisconsin–Green Bay. He is the author or coauthor of several nationally used standardized tests, textbooks on psychological testing and educational assessment, and more than 100 published articles and presentations related to psychological and educational measurement. He serves frequently as a consultant to government agencies, professional organizations, and businesses on matters of measurement, research design, and statistical analysis. He holds a bachelor's degree from John Carroll University and both a master's and a doctoral degree from Fordham University, with a specialization in psychometrics.

Chapter 1: Base R

R is a computer language with a particular orientation toward statistical uses. In its simplest form, R will operate like a calculator for you. At the next level, R has "functions" that will calculate statistics for you such as the mean and standard deviation. At the next higher level, R has "add-on packages" that are collections of routines for calculating more advanced statistics.

In this bare-bones introduction, we will try to accomplish four goals. First, we'll see how R works as a calculator. But we won't spend much time on that because it's kind of trivial. Next, we'll check out R's more common "functions," especially for elementary statistics—which is R's most important contribution for our purposes right now. Then, we'll introduce an especially important package, R Commander, that simplifies your use of R. Finally, we'll show how to get to other add-on packages and use them.

1–2 R'S UPS AND DOWNS

What are the ups and downs, the pluses and minuses of R? It has both. It has *three main advantages*:

1. First, it is free—completely. Just go to its home page (http://cran.r-project .org/) on the Internet and follow the directions for downloading. We'll walk through the download steps in the next section. You don't have to remember the home page address. Just Google R, and you'll easily get it.

Your initial download gives you "base R" and a few extra packages. Most important for our purposes, these include routines to calculate commonly used statistics, such as mean, standard deviation, and correlation, and to prepare commonly used graphs, such as the histogram and scatterplot.

2. Second, the R network includes "add-on packages" that provide a huge expansion in R applications. New packages are always being created, and this will continue indefinitely. Later, we describe how to add one of these packages and how to use it. All the add-on packages, as is true for base R, are free.

The most important of these add-on packages, for our purposes, is R Commander. While most of R requires us to "do programming," R Commander let's us do "point-and-click"—like what you do in Microsoft Word or Excel—and R Commander does the programming for us. You might ask, "If R Commander will do that for me, why should I learn anything else about R?" There are two reasons. First, some things are simpler to do in "base R." Second, when we get around to introducing R Commander, you'll find that a lot of what it does will not make much sense unless you have this bare-bones introduction to R itself.

3. Third, all parts of R are "open source," that is, you have access to the programming code, and you can change it if you want (with some restrictions so that you don't completely foul up the system). This feature offers a big advantage for experienced programmers. But it's not important for novices, the audience for this book.

R has *one big disadvantage*. Our benchmark for describing the disadvantage is commercially available statistical software, such as SPSS and Minitab, and even, to some extent, Microsoft Excel. In comparison with these packages, R is not very user-friendly. There is nothing intuitive about R. It has a lot of obscure terminology and customs. Output is not very elegant. Some of the output is just plain ugly—except for graphs, which are pretty cool. For the experienced programmer, R's enormous flexibility is great. For the casual user, it's very intimidating and mysterious. We'll deal with this problem in our "bare-bones" introduction. For those who want to go into R in more depth, there are plenty of other resources.

Of course, the commercially available packages also have their disadvantages, especially their cost. A commercial user, for example, will pay about a thousand bucks for SPSS, although there are some student discount versions, which you can rent for a semester for about a hundred bucks. The high cost, in turn, means that such packages are not widely available outside universities and major corporations. In addition, the commercially available packages are not open source.

1–3 GETTING STARTED: LOADING R

Let's get started. You need to have your computer connected to the Internet. Once you've downloaded R, you can use it without the Internet connection. Now, download R from one of its home pages (http://www.r-project.org/ or http://cran.r-project.org/). Copy one of these links into your browser. Or just Google "R," and you'll get to these sites.

Let's start with http://cran.r-project. Bring up that URL. You'll get a screen that starts with Figure 1.1.

Figure 1.1 Starting your download procedure

```
Download and Install R
```

Precompiled binary distributions of the base system and contributed packages, **Windows and Mac** users most likely want one of these versions of R:

- Linux
- MacOS X
- Windows

We're going to use the Windows operating system. Click on Windows.

That will bring up a screen starting with Figure 1.2. (Obviously, if you are on a Mac platform, click on Mac OS X and follow the succession of screens for Mac download, finally downloading R-2.9.1.dmg.)

Figure 1.2 Second step in download procedure

R for Windows

This directory contains binaries for a base distribution and packages to run on i386/x64 Windows.

Note: CRAN does not have Windows systems and cannot check these binaries for viruses. Use the normal precautions with downloaded executables.

Subdirectories:

| base | Binaries for base distribution (managed by Duncan Murdoch) |
| contrib | Binaries of contributed packages (managed by Uwe Ligges) |

Click on "base." That will bring up a screen that starts with Figure 1.3.

Figure 1.3   Third step in download procedure

R-2.9.0 for Windows

Download R 2.9.0 for Windows (36 megabytes)

Installation and other instructions
New features in this version: Windows specific, all platforms.

Then, click on "Download R-2.9.0 for Windows" (or the later version, when it becomes available). You don't need to read the "Installation and other instructions" (unless you want to get really technical).

R's installation procedures will now walk you through a series of screens. On each, you will choose the defaults, clicking Run, OK, or Next. Expert programmers may choose options other than the defaults—but not us. After working through these screens, you finally get to this: Figure 1.4.[1]

Figure 1.4   Finishing up your download

Click Finish, and you're done. The whole process takes only about 3 minutes.

---

[1]The screen shows version 2.9.2, released August 24, 2009.

❖ *A Little Wrinkle: The "Mirror" Site*

We started from http://cran.r-project. You can start from http://www.r-project/ org, then clicking on CRAN under Download Packages on the left side of the screen. If you do so, the procedure will first ask you to pick a "Mirror" site. Mirror sites appear around the globe. Just pick one near you, and click on it. When you do so, you'll get to exactly the same starting point as we used above. Proceed through the steps already described. We'll encounter this mirror site stuff again later.

Using the standard defaults will place the R icon on your desktop screen. Once it's there, double left click on the icon. This will bring up the R Console and the RGui (R graphical user interface; say R-Gui, where "Gui" rhymes with Huey, Louie, and Dewey!). Figure 1.5 shows what you get.

Figure 1.5 What you get when you open R by clicking on its icon

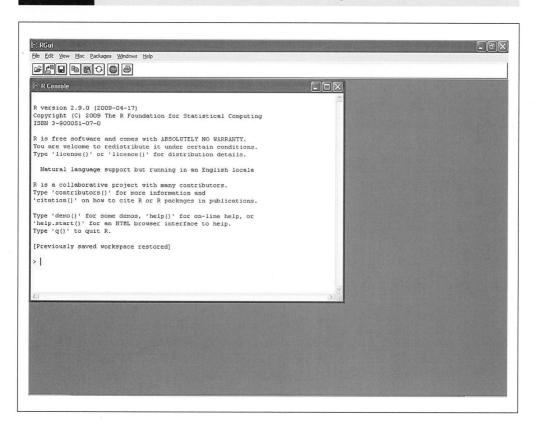

What we have downloaded is called "base R." Actually, several commonly used packages automatically come with it. Most important for our purposes, the "statistics" and "graphics" packages tag along.

Notice the ">" at the bottom of the R Console screen. This is called the R "prompt," by which R says, "I'm ready to do something. What would you like me to do?" Each time you do something by entering an instruction and hitting Enter or Return, your instruction will be executed, and another > prompt will appear; that is, R is ready for your next instruction. If R can't execute your instruction because it doesn't understand it, you'll get an error message, followed by another > prompt on the next line.

HT   Helpful Tip

> ⟵ This is the "R prompt."

It says R is ready to take your command.

1–4 GETTING STARTED REALLY: USING R AS A CALCULATOR

Now, let's do our first operation on R: just a simple calculation. Following the prompt, type in 2 + 3, then hit Enter (we'll assume you hit Enter at the end of each line we present in the following text):

```
>2+3
```

R will return this:

```
[1]  5

>
```

The 5 was no surprise, but the [1] was unexpected, right? It's just a line number, not useful when your result has only one line but useful for more complicated work where your result may span multiple lines. In that case, the line numbers help keep track of your work.

Notice also that after giving your result (5), R automatically presents another > prompt.

The box on the left shows R's commonly used operators for calculations. When using these, remember your rules for order of operations.

HT   Helpful Tip

Commonly Used Operators in R

+   addition

–   subtraction

*   multiplication

/   division

^   exponent

(e.g., 3^2 means 3 to second power or 3 squared)

NOTE: R has many other operators, but we use only those given here.

Now, try these to get a little more experience. Do these:

```
>2^3+(5)
>6/2+(8-5)
```

Before moving to the next level, let's note *three important conventions* in R:

1. First, it ignores blank spaces in your entries. For example,

```
>2^3+(5)
```

gives the same result as:

```
> 2 ^ 3 + (5)
```

2. Second, you can copy and paste commands in R just as you would in a word processor. This is particularly handy when you make a minor mistake in a command, you get an error message, and you want to reenter the command and then correct it. You can try the copy-and-paste procedure with one of the simple examples we have used so far. But don't copy the > prompt. If you do, you end up with a double prompt, such as this:

```
>>2^3+(5)
```

and R will scowl with an error message.

3. Third, you sometimes want to make a note to yourself about what you're trying to do with a command, although the note is not actually part of the command. To do this, to the right of the command line use the # sign, then enter your note. Here's an example:

HT **Helpful Tip**

⟵ This is the R notation symbol. Use it to put a note on a command.

```
>2^3+(5)     #I'm trying the exponent function
```

This is a pretty trivial example, but the # notation will become useful when we get to more complex examples.

Here's our first example for statistics. In the next section, we'll find a much simpler way to do this, but for now we're just using R like a calculator. Suppose we have these test scores for five cases (i.e., $n = 5$): 22, 34, 18, 29, 36. We calculate the average as:

```
> (22+34+18+29+36)/5   #Calculating the average, aka mean
```

Try it.

Do these calculations. Type the numbers and operators after the R prompt, then hit Enter. Observe the output:

```
26 - 1.97

158 + 104 + 98 + 85

26.4/(1.5 + 4.8)

2 ^ 5
```

1–5 CREATING A DATA SET

Now we start to get serious. So far, you've been saying, "It would be a lot simpler to do this stuff on my pocket calculator or on my cell phone—to heck with R." We will now use R to create a data set and then learn how to operate on that data set.

Let's use the test scores from above to create a data set called Scores. Here's how we do it:

```
>Scores=c(22, 34, 18, 29, 36)
```

The "c" stands for "concatenate"—an awful word here. It means, treat these entries as a data set.

Enter that command. Then, at the next >, simply type Scores, and hit Enter. You'll find that R has stored the test scores. Again, you'll notice the line number [1] and a new prompt. It looks like this:

```
>Scores

[1] 22 34 18 29 36

>
```

Here are five more *very* important notes.

First, what we just created (Scores) is called a "variable." Later on, we'll do a lot of work with variables.

Second, variable names are case sensitive. SCORES, scores, and Scores name three different variables. R enforces this case-sensitive feature mercilessly. Many error messages get generated by not observing this feature. Search engines often tolerate variation in cases and even in spellings. For example, you get pretty much the same result if you Google new york, NEW YORK, New York, or even New Yorkk. Not so with R. Get used to it.

Third, do not include blank spaces in variable names. For this reason, you will often see R data sets or file names with a period (.) or underscore (_) to join two words into a single name. For example, you might find Hogan.Data or Hogan_Data. Here you could also use HoganData, but don't use Hogan Data (notice the unwanted blank space between Hogan and Data). And don't use a dash (Hogan-Data); if you do, R will holler at you.

You might want to try some of the latter variations in variable names to see what happens.

Fourth, start your variable names with a letter. It can be either upper or lower case, but you need to remember which you used because the name is case sensitive.

Fifth, many sources, for example, some manuals and textbooks on R, use the symbols <- where we have used the equal sign (=) above. Thank heavens the equal sign works in the current version of R, although you can use <- if you want. Try it just once. For example,

```
>SCORES<-c(122, 134, 118, 129, 124)
```

At the next > prompt, type **SCORES**. You'll find (a) that <- worked like the equal sign and (b) that **SCORES** is different from Scores—remember, variable names are case sensitive. At the next >, type **Scores**, and you'll see that R still has the data values for **Scores**.

In a later section, we'll find another way to create a data set, especially for much larger data sets.

Our previous examples of data sets used only numerical information. Sometimes we have data that are nonnumerical, for example, alphabetical information such as names. R likes numerical information but is not fond of nonnumerical stuff. So if our data are, say, names, then we have to tell R to treat the stuff as nonnumerical by using quotation marks. It's a nuisance. Here's how it works to create a data set of five names, with the variable cleverly called **names**:

```
>names=c("Mary", "Tom", "Ed", "Dan", "Meg")
```

HT Helpful Tip

Variable names are case sensitive in R. Pay careful attention to this feature.

HT Helpful Tip

<- ⟵ Many sources use this notation where we have used the "=" sign.

HT Helpful Tip

' ' versus " "

R uses quotation marks in a lot of places.

You can always use either single (' ') or double (" ") quotation marks. Just be consistent, using either single or double, within a command.

Enter that, and at the next prompt just type **names.** You'll see that R has stored this nonnumerical data set.

✓**Self-Check 1–5**

Here are the heights in inches of six people:

72, 68, 76, 65, 59, 62

Use the "c" procedure to create a data set called **HTS.**
After creating it, at the next R prompt, type HTS to make sure your data are there.
The initials for the six people whose heights you recorded are

JT, BL, NA, CC, WR, JS.

Use the "c" procedure to create a data set called **HTS_Initials.**
Remember to use quote marks around each set of initials and put a comma between entries.

After creating it, at the next R prompt, type HTS_Initials to make sure the initials are there.

❖ *Saving Stuff*

You're not likely to get through this entire book in one sitting. Because we will use data sets created in early sections later on (and we don't want to re-create them), we want to save data sets for later use. It's easy to do so in R. You quit an R session either by typing quit ( ) at the > prompt or by just clicking the big X in the upper right corner of the R Console. When you do so, you'll get Figure 1.6.

Figure 1.6 Your screen when quitting an R session

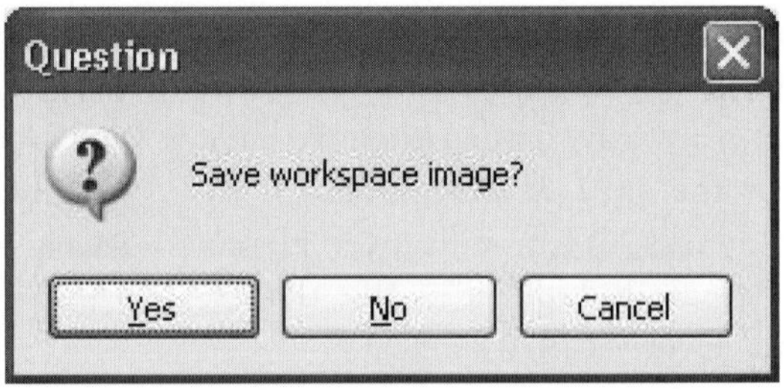

Just click on Yes. All your work will be saved. That work will be available when you next open R, provided you're on the same computer. It's a little scary the first time you log out of R, but you'll get used to it. After several sessions, you may get a bunch of "junk," and you'll want to get rid of some of it. We'll find how to do that in a later section.

1–6 USING R FUNCTIONS: SIMPLE STUFF

Now we come to one of the most important features of R. It has many built-in "functions." A function is a routine for accomplishing something, such as getting a mean, standard deviation, or correlation—the sorts of things we learn about in statistics. Once we have a data set in R, we use these functions to get statistics on the data set. We'll use the **Scores** data set we just created.

❖ *Commands for mean, sd, summary*

Here's our first example. Enter it.

```
>mean(Scores)
```

And, as you expected, R gives you the mean of your data set **Scores**.

Try it for **SCORES**.

Note that function names, like variable names, are case sensitive. Thus, to get the mean, use "mean," not "Mean" or "MEAN" or any other variation. As with variable names, R is merciless in enforcing this case-sensitive feature.

Now, try this to get the standard deviation:

```
>sd(Scores)
```

And here's a cute one. Try this:

```
>summary(Scores)
```

HT **Helpful Tip**

Saving Your Workspace

If you are working on a computer (e.g., your personal laptop) that allows you to save your work, the procedure just described works fine, and you can skip this box. However, if you are on a computer that does not allow you to save stuff to the hard drive (e.g., some university labs are set up this way), then you need to save your work to a different device, for example, to a flash drive.

Here is how to do so: On the RGui console, click on File (upper left corner), then on Save Workspace. Go to the device where you want to save the workspace (e.g., a flash drive), give the file a name, and hit Save.

When you next want to access the saved workspace, with RGui open, click on File, then Load Workspace. Go to the device where you saved the workspace, highlight the file, and click Open. Your saved workspace will open for your use.

Even if you have complete control of your computer for saving stuff, you can use the procedure just described to transfer your workspace between two computers, provided both have R.

HT **Helpful Tip**

Function names, like variable names, are case sensitive in R.

❖ *Command for correlation* (**cor**)

The correlation coefficient is another very popular statistic. R handles it nicely. Let's get the correlation between the two variables we just created: **Scores** and **SCORES**. Do this:

```
>cor(Scores, SCORES)
```

It returns the Pearson correlation coefficient. Later, we'll see how to do an entire correlation matrix, that is, the correlations among more than just two variables.

❖ *More Functions*

R contains hundreds of functions. We introduce only those most frequently encountered in introductory statistics. For a complete listing of the functions in the "stats" package that loads automatically with base R, go to the Help button on the toolbar of the RGui page, scroll to R functions (text), click, then enter one of the functions already introduced (e.g., sd). This will bring up a page with the right-hand side giving details of one function (e.g., sd) and the left-hand side showing the index of other functions. We'll do much more with a variety of functions in later sections (for a quick peek, see the table in the Helpful Tip box at the beginning of Section 1–11).

✓**Self-Check 1-6**

Recall the "heights" data set you created in Self-Check 1–5. Use the mean and sd functions to get the mean and standard deviation of the **HTS** data.

1–7 READING IN LARGER DATA SETS

The data sets we have used so far are rather trivial, although typical for those encountered in introductory statistics textbooks. In the real world, we usually have much larger data sets. We either create them from scratch or they already exist and we want to access them. Then, whether creating from scratch or accessing an existing file, we want to apply statistical techniques to them. In this section, we see how to do this. Let's consider a data set with six variables: ID, SEX (1 = *female*, 2 = *male*), State (1 = *PA*, 2 = *NY*, 3 = *NJ*; i.e., the student's state of home residence), SATV, SATM, and GPA for 20 students. The data set appears in Figure 1.7. SATV and SATM are SAT scores for verbal and math tests, and GPA is freshman year GPA. We note, first, that you could create this data set with a series of "c" commands. What a pain that would be!

Figure 1.7 Data for SATGPA20 file

ID	SEX	State	SATV	SATM	GPA
1	1	1	590	590	3.20
2	1	1	670	660	3.03
3	1	1	540	520	2.69
4	1	2	620	600	3.06
5	1	3	610	510	3.03
6	1	1	560	500	3.03
7	1	3	480	590	3.48
8	1	2	620	560	3.62
9	1	1	510	610	3.21
10	1	1	630	530	3.73
11	1	2	580	530	3.51
12	1	2	490	560	3.04
13	2	2	620	540	3.02
14	2	3	520	550	3.01
15	2	3	620	620	3.47
16	2	2	480	530	2.90
17	2	1	500	630	2.87
18	2	1	640	560	2.38
19	2	1	390	430	2.41
20	2	1	540	520	2.56

The more sensible way to create this data set is to put the data into an Excel file, an SPSS file, or even a Word document. You can, in fact, use any of these input methods and then read the data into R. We will do it with an Excel spreadsheet. (See Section 3–1 if you want to explore some other ways to do it.)

Open Microsoft Excel. In this spreadsheet, label the first column ID (for student ID, an arbitrarily assigned number), followed by each of our other five variables: SEX, State, SATV, SATM, and GPA. Then, enter the data. Save the spreadsheet as an Excel file. Let's call it **SATGPA20**. Or you may download the file (SATGPA20.xls) from the book's Web site at http://www.sagepub.com/Bare-BonesR.

With the Excel file open, save it as a text (Tab delimited) file. Click File, then Save As. Then, at the bottom of the save screen, where it says Save as Type, scroll to Text (Tab delimited), choose it, and hit Save. (You may need to click through a couple of warnings—just proceed, clicking Yes.)

Now you have the data saved as a text file, that is, with a .txt extension. Your original Excel file is still there with the .xls extension.

Next, we are ready to have R access the file. The one we want is the .txt version. We need to know its *exact path*. Where did you save it? Let's say you saved it on your E drive in a folder labeled R. So the path is E:/R/SATGPA20.txt for this file (don't forget the ".txt").

❖ The *read.table* Command

We will read the file (the table of data) with the read.table command. To use it, we first invent a name for the data set in R. We can still use **SATGPA20**, but let's add an R to it just to make the point that we're creating an R file. Then, do this:

```
>SATGPA20R=read.table("E:/R/SATGPA20.txt", header=T)
```

Here are a few quirks in this command:

1. Notice the quotation marks around the path name. Don't forget them.

2. Notice the comma after the close quotation mark.

3. What is that "header = T" thing? This tells R to read the first line (the header line) in the file as a set of variable names, provided you have T, which stands for TRUE. If you wanted R to read the first line not as a set of variable names but as regular data, use header = F. You guessed it—that's F for

FALSE. Actually, header = T is the default in the read.table command, so you don't have to include it. We've included it here just to make the point about the option you have on this matter. It's always OK to use T for TRUE or F for FALSE. It is *not* OK to use "True" or "False," or "true" or "false."

4. In R, when showing the exact path to a file, a forward slash (/) works the same as double backward slashes (\\).Thus, E:/R/SATGPA20.txt works the same as E:\\R\\SATGPA20.txt. You may be accustomed to single forward slashes. The file.choose ( ) command returns with double backward slashes and it's OK to use that format in the read.table command.

Let's use some commands we have used earlier to (a) make sure our data are available in R and (b) operate on the data with our functions.

To show that the data are there, do this:

```
>SATGPA20R
```

You should have a complete read-out of your data. (You probably would not want to do that if you have 50 variables for each of 5,000 cases!)

Remember the summary function. Try it, like this:

```
>summary(SATGPA20R)
```

Then, try this:

```
>mean(SATGPA20R)
```

❖ *The attach Command*

Here comes another quirky twist in R. Suppose you just want the mean of GPA in this data set. Try this:

```
>mean(GPA)
```

HT Helpful Tip

The file.choose Command

To have R access a file you need the file's exact path. Finding that exact path in the labyrinth of your computer system often presents a significant challenge. Fortunately, R has a clever, terribly useful command to help with the task. Type the command file.choose( ) following the R prompt. This opens up your system file menus, much like clicking on Open in any Microsoft application. Go find the file you want to open, and click on it. R will print the exact path to your file. Copy and paste this path, including the quotation marks, into the read.table command (see this section). If you already know the exact path to the file you want, you don't need the file.choose( ) command, but the command helps greatly when you don't know where the desired file is.

You get an error message, right? Here's what you have to do:

```
>attach(SATGPA20R)
```

Then, try this:

```
>mean(GPA)
```

Now you have the mean of just the GPA variable. And, of course, you can now get the mean of any variable, the standard deviation of any variable, the correlation between any two variables, and so on within this data set. Try this:

```
>cor(GPA,SATV)
```

✓ Self-Check 1–7.1

Go to the Web site for this book (http://www.sagepub.com/Bare-BonesR), and find the file SpatialData.txt. Download it to R using the `read.table` command. Call the new file **SpatialDataR.** Make sure you have it by typing **SpatialDataR** at the next prompt.

Then, use the `attach` command to allow access to individual variables in the data.

❖ The *data.frame* Command

Here's a command that is sort of in the same ballpark as the read.table command. Remember when we created a data set with the "c" command? Well, let's do a few "c" commands and then put all the data together in a "data frame." It's easy. Let's say we have created three data sets (IQ, Creativity Score, and Writing Quality for each of five students) as follows. Do these:

```
>IQ=c(110, 95, 140, 89, 102)
>CS=c(59, 40, 62, 40, 55)  #CS is Creativity Score
>WQ=c(2, 4, 5, 1, 3) #WQ is Writing Quality
```

Now, we'll put these three sets of scores together in a data frame called **All_Data,** like this:

```
>All_Data=data.frame(IQ, CS, WQ)
```

And by now, you should know what you'll get if you type **All_Data** at the next prompt. Do it:

```
>All_Data
```

And try this:

```
>mean(All_Data)
```

A little more practice. Do you still have the **Scores** and **names** data sets we created earlier? If so, do this, creating a new data frame called **Scores.and.names**:

```
>Scores.and.names = data.frame(names, Scores)
```

Then, enter:

```
>Scores.and.names
```

In the printout, notice that we got **names** to print first by putting it first in the data.frame command.

> ## ✓ Self-Check 1–7.2
>
> Recall the heights data set and initials data set you created in Self-Check 1–5. Use the data.frame command to combine these two data sets into a new data set called **HTSwithInitials.**

1–8 GETTING HELP

Let's pause, before introducing any new techniques, to see how to get help on R. It has pretty easy access to help menus, although—be forewarned—once you get to the help menus, they can be intimidating. They will usually present a whole lot more than what you need. We'll look at three ways to get help.

First, if you know the name of a function, for example, sd, do this:

```
>help(sd)
```

This brings up the formal description of how the sd function works. The description shows various options, defaults, some related functions, and so on.

Second, to get an example of the output for a function, say, sd, do this:

```
>example(sd)
```

This brings up an example of the output for the function entered in parentheses. Beware! Sometimes the examples present a bewildering array illustrating all or many of the options available for the function.

A third way to get help is to click the Help menu button on the RGui menu bar (at the top of the RGui). Do so. Notice that you can access R manuals—including one on all the methods for reading in (importing) data. The manuals are in pdf (portable document format) form. But bypass the manuals for now, and scroll to R functions (text) and click on it. You'll get a window where you can enter the name of a function. Enter mean and click OK. This brings up the formal definition of that function. Now notice that on the left side of the screen you have Contents and Index. You might want to scroll through these and try clicking on a few of the entries. The list seems endless, and many of the terms will be unfamiliar to you. All these functions reside in R, thus its great flexibility and power.

HT   Helpful Tip

R's "function" terms

R language: function (arguments)

Plain English: Do this (to this)

When you get to the Help menu for a particular function, you will see a reference to "arguments." Nobody's trying to pick a fight. Arguments are what a function operates on. A function does something. The arguments are what the function does it to, including any special conditions for doing it.

✓Self-Check 1–8

You want to find out how the *median* works in R. On the RGui, click on Help, then R functions (text). Enter "median" (without the quotation marks) and click OK. The R Help screen pops up. Observe its contents. Notice that na.rm = FALSE. We will deal with that in the next section. Notice also that your R Console shows >help("median"). Check that you get to the same place by typing directly in the R Console help(median), oddly with no quotation marks.

1–9 DEALING WITH MISSING DATA

All the sample data sets we have used so far have had complete data. However, many practical applications have some missing data. When some data are missing, we need to tell R what to do about it. The key phrase is na.rm, which says that when data are "not available, remove" them from the calculations. Let's try a couple of simple examples and see how this works. First, create this little data set:

```
>Data=c(2,4,6,NA,10)
```

Then, do this to show what you have:

```
>Data
```

Now, try this:

```
>mean(Data)
```

You get NA because R won't calculate a mean with the characters NA in the data set.

Now, do this:

```
>mean(Data, na.rm=T)
```

This tells R to calculate a mean after removing the NA values (i.e., na.rm = TRUE). Many statistical software packages, for example, SPSS and Excel, do this automatically. Dealing with NA is a big pain in the neck in R.

When creating a data set in R using any of the methods we have introduced (e.g., using Excel and then saving as a .txt file), you have to enter NA for missing data. You cannot just enter a blank or a space. And NA is case sensitive, so don't use "Na" or "na" (even though the command na.rm uses na!).

Let's add five cases with missing data to our SATGPA20 file, then save it as SATGPA25. Bring up your SATGPA20.xls file, and add the cases in Figure 1.8.

Figure 1.8   Add these data to SATGPA20, and save as SATGPA25

21	1	NA	NA	NA	3.14
22	1	2	480	580	2.80
23	2	1	NA	NA	2.68
24	2	1	470	520	3.28
25	2	NA	620	720	3.00

NOTE: NA = missing data.

Save it as an Excel file (SATGPA25.xls), then save it as a text file (SATGPA25.txt). Finally, bring it up as an R file, calling it **SATGPA25R,** like this:

```
>SATGPA25R=read.table("E:/R/SATGPA25.txt", header=T)
```

To make sure you created and read the file properly, do this:

```
>SATGPA25R
```

Then, do this:

```
>mean(SATGPA25R)
```

You got "NA" for those means that had missing data. So now do this:

```
>mean(SATGPA25R, na.rm=T)
```

Now, you have means for everything. Of course, the means for ID, SEX, and State are worthless because they are based on nominal scales. This emphasizes the point that you need to know what kind of data you have to make sense out of your results.

Unfortunately and unpredictably, na.rm does not work when using the correlation function (cor). Let's say you want to get the correlation between SATV and GPA in our **SATGPA25R** data set. Do this:

```
>cor(SATV, GPA, use='complete')
```

Similarly, if you want to get the complete correlation matrix for all variables in SATGPA25R, do this:

```
>cor(SATGPA25R, use='complete')
```

Of course the correlations involving the ID, SEX, and State variables don't make much sense here. But we're just trying to show how to deal with missing data.

1–10 USING R FUNCTIONS: HYPOTHESIS TESTS

Don't do this section unless you have already been introduced to hypothesis testing, especially the *t* test and chi-square. We'll proceed on the assumption that you know what these tests are for and generally how they work.

Let's work with our **SATGPA25R** file. To make sure that file is accessible, use our attach command, like this:

```
>attach(SATGPA25R)
```

❖ *The t test*

Suppose we want to test the hypothesis that the means for females (*F*) and males (*M*) are equal for SATM (formally, H_0: $\mu_F = \mu_M$). Here's the command:

```
>t.test(SATM~SEX)
```

The funny little symbol between SATM and SEX is the tilde, found on the left-hand side of the top row of many keyboards (upper case). You can read this as "Do a *t* test on SATM by SEX."

After entering the above command, the R Console shows this output:

```
Welch Two Sample t-test

data: SATM by SEX

t=0.0936, df=13.682, p-value=0.9268

alternative hypothesis: true difference in means is
not equal to 0

95 percent confidence interval:

-57.45245 62.68322

sample estimates:

mean in group female mean in group male

564.6154     562.0000
```

R contains lots of variations in the command for the *t* test. The simple form we just introduced has used several "defaults." A default means that R makes certain assumptions about how you want to execute a command. You can change these assumptions by adding to the command. Among the assumptions we used by default in the *t* test we just did are that (a) we wanted a two-sided alternative hypothesis, (b) the variances were not necessarily equal, and (c) the samples were independent, as opposed to paired. In effect, by default, built into our simple command above were these statements: alt = "two.sided," var.equal = FALSE, and paired = FALSE.

Let's do the same *t* test but with the assumption that variances are equal. Do this:

```
>t.test(SATM~SEX, var.equal=TRUE)
```

Check the difference in your output on the R Console for this versus the previous command.

For a one-sided *t* test, use alt = "less" or alt = "greater" (including the quotation marks) depending on which direction you want your alternative hypothesis to go.

Finally, here's how to do a paired- or dependent-samples *t* test. Let's say we want to test SATV versus SATM for our 25 cases. These are two different measures on the same cases, so the situation calls for a paired-samples test. The command goes like this:

```
>t.test(SATV, SATM, paired=T)
```

Notice that we have used T here instead of TRUE, which we used in the preceding example. It's always OK to use T for TRUE or F for FALSE.

By the way, in all the output for these *t* tests, the confidence interval (CI) is around the difference between means. And, by default, it's a 95% CI. Want to change to, say, 99% CI? Include in the command conf.level = 0.99, thereby changing the default.

Interestingly, R has enough sense to ignore missing data (those NA entries) when doing a *t* test. You don't have to include any special instruction (such as na.rm or use = 'complete') to do a *t* test when some data are missing.

> ✓ **Self-Check 1–10**
>
> Use the **SATGPA25R** data set to test the hypothesis that males and females are equal in GPA. Use the *t* test, assuming equal variances.

❖ Chi-Square

Another commonly used hypothesis test is the chi-square (χ^2). Recall that we use it to test for dependency between two nominal-scale variables. We have two such variables in the **SATGPA25R** file: SEX and State. In the usual tabular form, the data look like this:

```
            PA        NY        NJ
   Female    6         5         2
   Male      6         2         2
```

Are these variables related? Or are they independent of one another? We apply R's chi-square test like this:

```
>chisq.test (SEX, State)
```

Enter that in your R Console. It yields the following:

```
Pearson's Chi-squared test

data: SEX and State

X-squared=0.9099, df=2, p-value=0.6345

Warning message:

In chisq.test(SEX, State): Chi-squared approximation
may be incorrect
```

The warning occurs because some cells in the two-way table have very small frequencies, which chi-square doesn't like. Disregarding that point, we note a *p* value (.6345) well above the .05 level. So we conclude that there is (probably) no relationship between SEX and State, a conclusion clearly consistent with simple observation of the tabular data.

As you might expect, R contains functions for doing analysis of variance. But we delay introducing it until later—although for sure you're dying to try it.

1–11 R FUNCTIONS FOR COMMONLY USED STATISTICS

R contains hundreds of statistical functions. We list here just those most commonly covered in introductory statistics textbooks. To see additional functions, use the Help, then R functions (text) . . . menu on the R Console.

HT	Helpful Tip	
List of R Functions for Commonly Used Statistics		
Function	*Calculates This*	*See Notes*
mean ( )	mean	1
median ( )	median	1
mode ( )	mode	1
sd ( )	standard deviation	1
range ( )	range	1
IQR ( )	interquartile range	1

(Continued)

(Continued)

Function	Calculates This	See Notes
min ( )	minimum value	1
max ( )	maximum value	1
cor ( )	correlation	2
quantile ( )	a percentile	3
t.test ( )	performs t-test	4
chisq.test ( )	performs chi-square	4

NOTES:

1. Insert the name of the variable *or* data set in parentheses.

   Remember to use na.rm = T, if needed.

2. Insert two or more variables or the entire data set.

   See notes in text about missing data.

3. In parentheses, give the variable name and the quantile with a decimal

   (e.g., 0.25).

4. See text for what to enter in parentheses.

✓ **Self-Check 1–11**

For the **SATGPA25R** data set, find

the range for GPA,

the 25th quantile for SATM, and

the correlation between SATV and SATM

1–12 TWO COMMANDS FOR MANAGING YOUR FILES

R has a plethora of ways to manage your files. Two of these are particularly helpful.

First, after you have worked with R for a bit, you'll probably accumulate a lot of data sets. And you won't remember what you've saved. To check, do this:

```
>ls ( )
```

It will return a list of your saved files.

Second, you may want to remove a file that you no longer need. Do this, inserting the name of the file in the parentheses:

```
>rm(file)
```

After doing that, again do this:

```
>ls( )
```

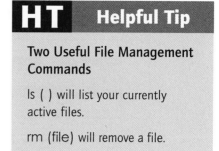

HT   **Helpful Tip**

Two Useful File Management Commands

ls ( ) will list your currently active files.

rm (file) will remove a file.

You'll see that the name of the file you used with rm is gone.

If you're fed up with R's annoying abbreviations, you can use remove (file) here instead of rm (file). Alas, list ( ) will not work in place of ls ( ).

You can use rm (file) to remove either a data file or a function you have custom-built (see Section 3–3).

✓**Self-Check 1–12**

Use the ls ( ) command to list your current R files.

Pick one of the files we no longer need (e.g., **HTS**), and remove it.

Again use ls ( ) to verify that HTS is gone.

1–13 R GRAPHICS

So far we have only done calculations in R—for example, calculating the mean and standard deviation. R can also prepare graphs, for example, histograms, boxplots, and scatterplots. Let's start with histograms and boxplots. Make sure you have your **SATGPA25R** file available.

❖ The **hist** and **boxplot** Commands

Doing histograms and boxplots is really easy in R. Let's get the histogram for SATM like this:

```
>hist(SATM)
```

A new window, the R Graphics window, pops up with the histogram (Figure 1.9). The Graphics package will automatically scale the axes to yield a reasonable graph. Later, we will see how you can change the axes.

Figure 1.9   Your first graph in R

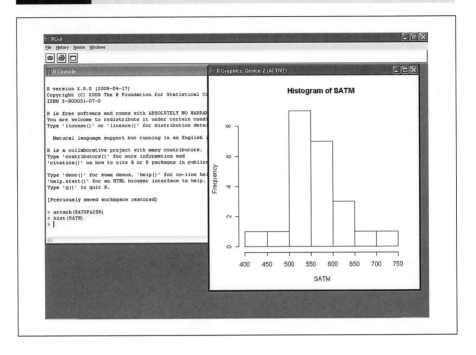

We get the boxplot of SATM like this:

```
>boxplot(SATM)
```

We can get a comparison of the boxplots for SATV and SATM like this:

```
>boxplot(SATV, SATM)
```

Here's a very nice feature of the R Graphics package. Remember what a pain it was to deal with missing data in the "stats" package? The Graphics package doesn't mind missing data. It will do what you'd expect it to do—disregard missing data. Recall that we had missing data for both our SATV and SATM variables, but the histograms and boxplots worked fine without doing anything about the missing data.

✓**Self-Check 1–13.1**

Get the histogram and boxplot for the GPA variable in the **SATGPA25R** file.

❖ *The plot Command*

Let's do a scatterplot (aka bivariate distribution). Let's define two variables, RS (a reading test score) and MS (a math test score), using the "c" function:

```
>RS=c(12,14,16,18,25)

>MS=c(10,8,16,12,20)
```

Do this to assure yourself that you have correctly stored the values for RS and MS:

```
>RS

>MS
```

Now, do this:

```
>plot(RS, MS)
```

It brings up a scatterplot in your Graphics window.

❖ *Getting the Line of Best Fit*

Recall that we often want to see the "line of best fit" in the scatterplot. Getting this is not entirely obvious, but here's a way to do it. First, do this:

```
>lm(MS~RS)        #lm means linear model
```

The "lm" function applies the "linear model" to predicting MS from RS. There's our little tilde again.

Then, get the "residuals" for this linear model, and store them in "res" (you can call it something else if you want) like this:

```
>res=lm(MS~RS) #res means residuals
```

Then, do this:

```
>abline(res)     #read as 'a-b' line
```

Don't pronounce "ab" as rhyming with *nab* or *lab*. Rather, pronounce it as "a-b" because it is using the values of "a" and "b" in the well-known equation $Y' = a + bX$ to predict Y from X (where a is the intercept and b is the slope of the best-fitting line). In our example, MS is the Y variable, and RS is the X variable. And the "abline" function will insert the best-fitting line into our scatterplot of MS and RS.

Do it, then check the scatterplot. If you got all the steps right, you should have the best-fitting line.

> ✓ **Self-Check 1–13.2**
>
> In the **SATGPA25R** file, predict GPA from SATM. First, prepare the plot, then insert the line of best fit.

❖ Controlling Your Graphics: A Brief Look

As noted earlier, R does a reasonable job of setting up your graph. It does this with a set of defaults—the usual way of doing something. However, you can override these defaults if you want to change the appearance of your graph. R has a veritable cornucopia of ways to make the changes; none of them are obvious, and some of them don't even work the same way from one type of graph to another. We will introduce just a few of the options for changing your graphs. We do so mainly to illustrate how they work. Then, we'll refer you to other sources for more complete coverage.

Let's start with the plot command. By default, it will scale the x-axis and y-axis to cover the lowest and highest values on each variable. Let's work with the reading and math test scores, RS and MS. In the plot we just created, the RS axis (the x-axis) went from 12 to 24. The MS axis (the y-axis) went from 8 to 20. Suppose you want both sets of axes to go from 5 to 25. Do this:

```
>plot(RS, MS, xlim=c(5,25), ylim=c(5,25))
```

This says, "Use limits of 5 to 25 for both RS and MS." Try it and see what you get in comparison with just:

```
>plot(RS, MS)
```

You might want to experiment with other "limits" for the two variables to see how your plot changes. By the way, be sure to use the double close parentheses at the end of the command.

Now, here's another variation. You can change the characters used in your plot.

The default is the little circles you saw in your first plot. Want to change them to, say, little crosses? Use the *pch* function, which stands for "print character." (We warned you this wasn't very intuitive.) Add this to your plot command:

```
>plot(RS, MS, pch=3)
```

Somewhere hidden in R's memory it knows that 3 means little crosses for *pch*. R has a host of *pch* equivalencies, too many for us to cover here. To pursue this, try this:

```
>help(pch)
```

Here's another: line width, abbreviated as *lwd*. It will change the width of characters. So try this:

```
>plot(RS, MS, pch=3, lwd=5)
```

Compare the result with your previous graphs. To show the complexity of using these options in R, the *lwd* option works differently for the plot command and the histogram (hist) command. In plot, it changes the data points plotted. In hist, it changes the thickness of the *x*- and *y*-axes.

And here's one more. You can replace the labels on the axes with *xlab* and *ylab*. Try this:

```
>plot(RS, MS, xlab="Reading Score", ylab="Math Score")
```

Be sure to put the new labels in quotation marks.

We have used the limits (*lim*), labels (*lab*), line width (*lwd*), and print character (*pch*) controls in separate commands. You can use them all in one command. Just separate them with commas. Try this:

```
>plot(RS, MS, pch=3, lwd=5, xlim=c(5,25), ylim=c(5,25),
xlab="Reading Score", ylab="Math Score")
```

That's enough to illustrate that you can exercise some control over your graphs, but it's not simple. To pursue this topic, see Chapter 12 in the official manual for R on the R home page (http://cran.r-project.org/) and an entire book just on R graphics (Murrell, 2005).

✓ Self-Check 1–13.3

Make a new plot for the one you prepared in Self-Check 1–13.2 (plotting GPA and SATM) with these changes:

Make the *Y*-axis (GPA) go from 2.0 to 4.0.

Label the *X*-axis "SAT Math."

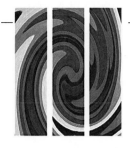

Chapter 2: R Commander

R Commander is a very important package in the R system, especially for casual users like us. It provides a version of R that operates much like the widely used statistical software packages, for example, SPSS and Minitab. For sure, you will ask, "If R has a version like, say, SPSS, why did you just put me through all that stuff about prompts, functions, read.table, and so on?" Good question. There are two answers. First, you probably would not understand how R Commander works unless you know something about *base R* commands. Once you start using R Commander, you'll see a lot of output showing base R commands; and how you use data sets in R Commander follows from how you use them in base R. Second, R Commander itself is an add-on package, so you need to know how to load a package in base R to get to R Commander.

❖ *Loading R Commander (Rcmdr)*

Let's do it. R Commander, abbreviated as *Rcmdr*, is one of R's "add-on" packages. So we need to follow the steps for getting such a package. You need an Internet connection to load a new package. Once loaded onto your computer, you don't need the Internet connection to use the package. There are several ways to install an add-on package. Here's the simplest way:

1. With your RGui open, click on Packages at the top of the screen (big surprise, eh?).

2. In the drop-down menu, click on (another big surprise) Install package(s). This brings up a list of "CRAN mirror" sites. These are sites scattered around the world that serve as repositories of R stuff.

3. Scroll to a mirror site near you, highlight it, and then click OK.

4. Now you will get a list of all the add-on packages.

5. Scroll to the package you want (in our case *Rcmdr*), highlight it, and then click OK.

6. The R Console should show that your package has been downloaded.

7. However, the package is not ready for use until you do this:

```
>library(Rcmdr)
```

That command activates the package in your library. When you execute this command, you'll get this scary message (Figure 2.1):

Figure 2.1   Message when you first activate Rcmdr

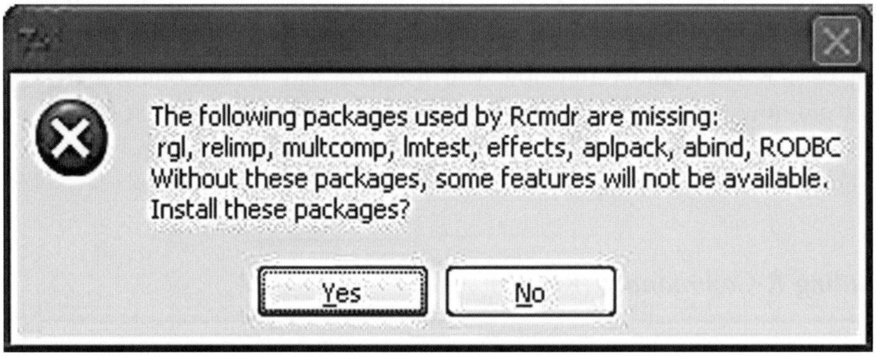

Not to worry. You haven't done anything wrong. Just click on "Yes," then OK on the next screen, and these other packages will download. Be forewarned—the downloading will take about 5 minutes. Time to take a break!

You can use some features of R Commander without these other packages (thus clicking No in the last screen), but we want these other packages available. You download these packages to your computer only once, not every time you access R Commander.

To make sure you have R Commander available for use, do this:

```
>library( )
```

That command lists all the packages currently active in your library. Make sure *Rcmdr* is there because we are now going to use it. Provided everything worked OK, the last command will bring up the R Commander window (Figure 2.2).

Figure 2.2 The R Commander opening window

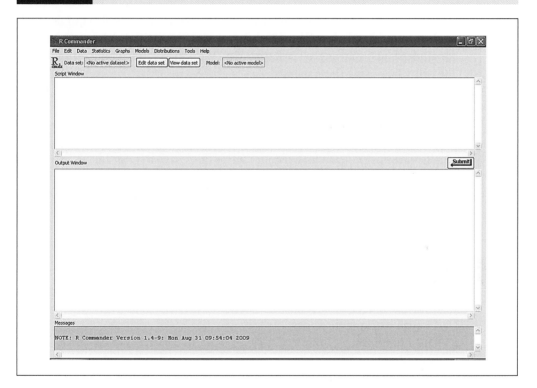

2–2 R COMMANDER WINDOWS AND MENUS

Before operating with R Commander, let's look over what we have here. Notice two blank parts of the screen, one labeled Script Window, the other labeled Output Window. Once we start "doing statistics" in R Commander, the Script Window will list the commands executed. They will look like the commands we used earlier in base R. More obviously, the

Output Window will contain the output, that is, the results of our statistical operations. And the output will look like what we got in base R (and as with base R, it's not very elegant). The Messages window at the bottom will contain those dreaded error messages that come up when you foul up something.

Now let's look at the menus across the top of the R Commander screen:

```
File, Edit, Data, Statistics, Graphs, Models,
Distributions, Tools, Help
```

For the most part, you can guess what drop-down menus you'll get under each of these menu headings, although there are a few surprises and imponderables for students just starting to learn statistics. We will describe half a dozen things for you when using these menus.

The menus of most interest to us for elementary statistics are **Data**, **Statistics**, and **Graphs**. We'll concentrate on these—in just a moment. Let's first comment on the other menu headings and their drop-down menus.

File (see Table 2.1) works like the File menu in Microsoft. It allows you to change directories, open an existing "script file," save a script file, save output, and save workspace. A script file is a set of R commands, created either in base R or in R Commander. The output is—right, you guessed it—output from R Commander; and workspace is your R workspace.

Table 2.1	Master List of Menus and Submenus Under File in R Commander

Change working directory
Open script file
Save script
Save script as
Save output
Save output as
Save R workspace
Save R workspace as
Exit   { From Commander
                    From Commander and R

Edit (see Table 2.2) works much like Edit in Microsoft. Use it to cut, copy, paste, and so on. You can do all these things with a right click on your mouse, so you don't really need the Edit menu.

Table 2.2	Master List of Menus and Submenus Under Edit in R Commander

Cut
Copy
Paste
Find
Select all
Undo
Redo
Clear window

Models has a lot of stuff for more advanced statistics, so for the most part we'll ignore it. Ditto for **Distributions**. You can look at the menus for both Models and Distributions, but we'll not use them, with one tiny exception later.

Tools provides another way to "Load package(s)" but we've already covered that so will not do so again; and there's an "Options" menu to change some things, such as font sizes on the Output Window, but we'll leave those at their default values.

Help, obviously, provides access to some help, specifically a searchable index and an introduction to R Commander.

Now let's go back to the three menus of most use for introductory statistics: **Data, Statistics,** and **Graphs.**

2–3 THE DATA MENU

Table 2.3 shows a master list of menus and submenus under **Data.** (This is really important stuff!) At present, the R Commander window is showing <No active data set>, and if you click on Edit data set or View data set, it just beeps at you.

Table 2.3	Master List of Menus and Submenus Under Data in R Commander

New data set

Load data set

Import data
- from text file, clipboard, or URL
- from SPSS data set
- from Minitab data set
- from STATA data set
- from Excel, Access, or dBase data set

Data in packages
- List data sets in packages
- Read data set from an attached package

Active data set
- Select active data set
- Refresh active data set
- Help on active data set (if available)
- Variables in active data set
- Set case names
- Remove row(s) from active data set
- Stack variables in active data set
- Remove cases with missing data
- Save active data set
- Export active data set

Manage variables in active data set
- Recode variables
- Compute new variable
- Add observation numbers to data set
- Standardize variables
- Convert numeric variables to factors
- Bin numeric variables
- Reorder factor levels
- Define contrasts for a factor
- Rename variables
- Delete variables from active data set

Let's comment on each option in the drop-down menu and actually use a few of them.

❖ *New data set*

New data set opens a new window that allows you to enter data. It looks much like an Excel or SPSS spreadsheet. Let's do it. At the top of the R Commander window, click Data, then New data set. A box opens for you to name the data set. Let's call it **SampleData**. Enter that name, remove the default name (Dataset), then click OK. (Remember file name conventions: Start with a letter, no spaces, case sensitive.) After clicking OK, the spreadsheet opens. It looks like Figure 2.3.

Figure 2.3	R Commander's spreadsheet (New data set)

	var1	var2	var3	var4	var5	var6	var7	var8
1								
2								
3								
4								
5								
6								
7								
8								
9								
10								
11								
12								
13								
14								
15								
16								
17								
18								
19								
20								

Let's enter the following small data set:

var1	var2	var3
2	1	5
5	4	7
3	7	8
6	8	9
9	2	9

HT   Helpful Tip

When navigating around R Commander's New data set spreadsheet, use your arrow keys or your mouse cursor. Don't use the TAB key. If you do, bad things may happen.

Kill this window by clicking on the "X" in the upper right corner of the spreadsheet. Don't worry, R Commander is saving your data set as **SampleData**.

Now, notice that **SampleData** appears as the active data set. You can View data set (just click on it). You can Edit data set (click on it, and change or add data).

You can also now operate on this data set. Let's try it. Recall the way to get means. In the Script window, type

```
mean(SampleData)
```

The line will *not* start with the > prompt. After typing mean (**SampleData**), click on the Submit button sitting to the right between the Script Window and the Output Window.

The Output Window will show the complete command, including the > prompt, and will give the means of the variables in **SampleData**. For practice, you can also try this:

```
sd(SampleData)
```

Now, recall the attach command. The variables in **SampleData** are labeled var1, var2, and var3. In the Script Window, type:

```
mean(var1)
```

and hit Submit.

You get an error message (in the Message box at the bottom) and no mean for var1. Now, in the Script Window type:

```
attach(SampleData)
```

and hit Submit. Then, again type:

```
mean(var1)
```

Hit Submit, and you'll get the mean of var1.

❖ *Changing "var" Names*

Two more things before moving on. Our variable names (var1, var2, var3), assigned by default, are not very helpful. Let's say the variables are three raters who provided ratings of the quality of artistic products. We want our variables to be Rater1, Rater2, and Rater3.

Click on Data, then Manage variables in active data set, and then Rename variables. A new window labeled Rename Variables appears. Highlight var1, var2, and var3; then, click OK. Insert the new names, and click OK. Now, again type:

```
mean(SampleData)
```

and hit Submit, and you'll find the new variable names are now used for the output.

Also, try this:

```
mean(Rater1)
```

You get the mean for Rater1. R remembered that you changed the variable name, and you do not have to use the attach command again.

Suppose we want to create a variable called Total, which is the sum of the three ratings. Click on Data, then Manage variables in active data set, and then Compute new variable. A new window opens, cleverly labeled Compute New Variable. Enter a name for the new variable, we'll call it Total. In the box for Expression to compute, enter Rater1+Rater2+Rater3. (You can type it directly or use highlighting and double clicking to move in variable names.) After hitting OK, click the View data set button and you'll see your newly created variable. You might again try this:

```
mean(SampleData)
```

You'll find that you now get means for Rater1, Rater2, Rater3, and Total.

Notice that Manage variables in active data set also allows you to do some other things with variables, but we will not go into those now.

❖ *Load data set; Data in packages*

Load data set allows you to load a data set already created in R. The data set must be in .rda format. If you have such a file, you can use this command. We will not pursue it here. Similarly, we will not pursue **Data in packages**. As suggested by its title, this allows you to access data sets in various add-on packages.

❖ *Import data*

The **Import data** menu is *very important*. It allows us to access data sets that already exist in text files (.txt), Microsoft Excel or Access, and several statistical software packages. Import data will read the data in any of these file formats and convert it to an R spreadsheet. Let's try it, using the **SATGPA25** we created earlier as a text file. It's pretty easy. Click Data, then Import data, then from text file, clipboard, or URL. This brings up a new window. Give the data set a name; we'll continue to use **SATGPA25R**. All the defaults in the remainder of this window are acceptable, but change them if necessary.

Hit OK. Then, you need to go find the file in your system. We had saved it in our E:/R folder. Get to it, and click on it. It will now appear as your active data set. You can check that by clicking on View data set.

Where did **SampleData** go? Click on Data, then Active data set, and then Select active data set. A new window appears, showing the data sets currently available. If you want to go back to **SampleData,** just click on it. It will now show up as your active data set. Of course, you can follow the same procedures and reactivate **SATGPA25R.**

If you have an existing Excel file handy, you might try accessing it with the Import data routine. You don't have to save it first as a text file, as we had to do when using base R.

We want to move next to the **Statistics** menu—the one you have really been waiting for. That's the one, as you might expect, that allows us to do many of the basic statistical procedures. However, before proceeding to the Statistics menu, we need to take a little detour.

❖ *Convert Numeric Variables to Factors*

Recall from your introductory statistics course the distinctions among types of scales: nominal, ordinal, interval, and ratio. The most important of these distinctions, for our present purposes, is the one between the nominal scale and the other three scales. The nominal scale simply classifies objects, for example, into male and female; those who prefer baseball, football, or basketball; or people who live in the Northeast, Southeast, Midwest, or far West. None of these classifications has any quantitative dimension. All the other scales (ordinal, interval, ratio) have an underlying quantitative continuum.

When we enter data into R, it assumes that the data are numeric with an underlying continuum; that is, it assumes that the data are ordinal, interval, or ratio. If we want R to treat a variable as nominal, we need to tell it to do so. In R Commander, such a variable is known as a factor. For example, in our **SATGPA25R** file, we want to use the SEX and State variables as nominal variables, that is, as factors. Doing so will become important when we want to perform certain statistical operations, such as a *t* test contrasting male and female performance on SATV or GPA (both of which are numeric variables).

To make the conversion, first, bring up the **SATGPA25R**, using Data, then Active data set, and then select the **SATGPA25R** file. Now, again go to Data, then Manage variables in active data set, and Convert numeric variables to factors. Highlight the variable(s) you want to convert—in our case, the SEX and State variables—and click OK. In the next window, give labels to the levels of the variable. You don't have to do so, but we will: For SEX, call value 1 female and value 2 male, and click OK; for State, call value 1 PA, value 2 NY, and value 3 NJ, and click OK. To check on your conversion, click on View data set.

One other thing: We don't want to clutter up our output with calculations on the ID variable, so let's get rid of it in the R data set. (It will still be in the original data file in case we ever want it.) Do this: Data, then Manage variables in active data set, and Delete variables from data set. Highlight "ID," and click OK.

✓ Self-Check 2–3

On the Data menu, use the New data set submenu to create the data set called **MyData:**

var1	var2	var3	var4
1	18	1	65
2	20	1	73
3	21	1	84
4	NA	2	60
5	21	2	98
6	17	2	77

After entering the data, click the "X" in the upper right corner of the spreadsheet. Then, make sure **MyData** shows in the Data set box. Click on View data set to see your data.

(Continued)

(Continued)

Now, go to Data, Manage variables in active data set, Rename variables, and rename the variables as follows: var1 is ID, var2 is Age, var3 is Gender, and var4 is TestScore.

Then, go to Data, Manage variables in active data set, Convert numeric variables to factors, and change ID and Gender to "factors," with 1 = *Boy* and 2 = *Girl* for Gender. Again, click on View data set to see your data.

2–4 THE STATISTICS MENU

At last, we get to the **Statistics** menu. We will use this menu to calculate many of the statistics covered in an introductory statistics course. Of course, we already know how to do some of these in base R. But R Commander will simplify life for us. Table 2.4 shows the menus and submenus for Statistics.

Table 2.4	Master List of Menus and Submenus Under Statistics in R Commander

Summaries	Active data set
	Numerical summaries
	Frequency distributions
	Count missing observations
	Table of statistics
	Correlation matrix
	Correlation test
	Shapiro-Wilk test of normality
Contingency tables	Two-way table
	Multi-way table
	Enter and analyze two-way table

Means	Single-sample t-test Independent samples t-test Paired t-test One-way ANOVA Multi-way ANOVA
Proportions	Single-sample proportion test Two-samples proportions test
Variances	Two-variances F-test Bartlett's test Levene's test
Nonparametric tests	Two-sample Wilcoxon test Paired-samples Wilcoxon test Kruskall-Wallis test Friedman rank-sum test
Dimensional analysis	Scale reliability Principal components analysis Factor analysis Cluster analysis
Fit models	Linear regression Linear model Generalized linear model Multinomial logit model Ordinal regression model

Let's comment on each entry in the table, and try some of them. With just a little experience, you'll navigate through these menus easily—at least for those statistics you've already learned about. Be aware that the titles for some of the menus and submenus are not very descriptive of what they actually do or, worse, are sometimes positively misleading. For example, you'd think the **Means** menu would give you means, but actually it's where you find the *t* test and analysis of variance. Some of the menus contain only procedures for more advanced statistical topics, and we will not cover those topics.

To use the Statistics menu, you need to have an active data set in your R Commander window. Let's use the **SATGPA25R** file. If you saved it when we created it in R, you can access it by going to the Data menu, then Active data set, and then Select active data set. Highlight SATGPA25R, and click OK. Notice that it now appears in the little box after Data set.

The **Summaries** option contains a lot of what you cover in introductory statistics. See the preceding table for its submenus, which we'll now walk through.

❖ *Active data set*

Hit Active data set, and it will give you this:

```
> summary(SATGPA25R)
   SEX        State      SATV             SATM             GPA
 female:14  PA  :12  Min.    :390.0  Min.    :430.0  Min.    :2.380
 male  :11  NY  : 7  1st Qu. :495.0  1st Qu. :525.0  1st Qu. :2.870
            NJ  : 4  Median :560.0   Median :560.0   Median :3.030
            NA's: 2  Mean    :555.7  Mean    :563.5  Mean    :3.046
                     3rd Qu. :620.0  3rd Qu. :595.0  3rd Qu. :3.210
                     Max.    :670.0  Max.    :720.0  Max.    :3.730
                     NA's    : 2.0   NA's    : 2.0
```

That is, you get a count on the nominal variables (the "factors") and for each of the continuous variables, the minimum, the maximum, 1st and 3rd quartiles, the median, and the mean. Oddly, it does not give you the standard deviation. The output is the same as what you would have obtained in base R with the command >summary(SATGPA25R), as indicated by the Output Window and the Script Window. As with the output from base R, the R Commander output is not pretty. Notice that the output shows the number of missing data points (NAs). You didn't have to tell R Commander what to do about missing data.

❖ *Numerical summaries*

Next, under Statistics, then Summaries, go to Numerical summaries (Figure 2.4).

Figure 2.4	The **Numerical summaries** screen

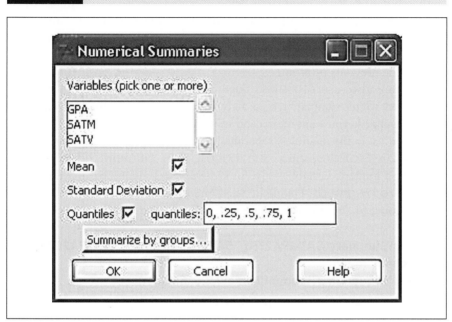

You find only the "numeric" variables available. In our **SATGPA25R** data set, these are GPA, SATM, and SATV. Our SEX and State variables do not appear, because they are now "factor" (i.e., nonnumeric) variables. **Numerical summaries** allows us to do several things. First, we can use the default settings (notice that defaults are checked) to get the mean, standard deviation, and the quantiles 0, .25, .5, .75, and 1 for one or more of the numeric variables. To do so, highlight the variables of interest. Let's do it for all three numeric variables. Click Statistics, then Summaries, and then Numerical summaries; then highlight GPA, SATM, and SATV, and click OK. You get this:

```
>   numSummary(SATGPA25R[,c("GPA",   "SATM",   "SATV")],
statistics=c("mean", "sd",
  +   "quantiles"), quantiles=c(0,.25,.5,.75,1))
```

	mean	sd	0%	25%	50%	75%	100%	n	NA
GPA	3.0460	0.3510579	2.38	2.87	3.03	3.21	3.73	25	0
SATM	563.4783	60.7235686	430.00	525.00	560.00	595.00	720.00	23	2
SATV	555.6522	72.1000622	390.00	495.00	560.00	620.00	670.00	23	2

Notice how R Commander prints out, in both the Script Window and the Output Window, the R commands being executed. Notice also that, although you did not request it, the printout contains *n* (the number of active data points) and NA (the number of missing data points). The 0% quantile is the same as the minimum (min), and the 100% quantile is the maximum (max) given in the previous printout.

You can also use Statistics, then Summaries, and then Numerical summaries to get summaries separately for any of your factor variables. For example, suppose you want means and standard deviations on GPA, SATM, and SATV (we'll skip the quantiles) separately for female and male cases. Do this:

Click on Statistics, then Summaries, then Numerical summaries. Highlight a numeric variable—say, SATM—uncheck quantiles, and then click Summarize by groups. Highlight SEX, and click OK. It will now show that you are going to "Summarize by SEX." Click OK. Here's what you get:

```
> numSummary(SATGPA25R[,"SATM"], groups=SATGPA25R$SEX,
statistics=c("mean",
+ "sd", "quantiles"), quantiles=c(0,.25,.5,.75,1))
```

	mean	sd	n	NA
female	564.6154	46.11858	13	1
male	562.0000	78.57056	10	1

Oddly, the summary of the command still lists quantiles, although they do not print out. Notice, again, that you automatically get *n* (number of active data points) and NA (number of missing data points—we had missing SATM for one female and one male).

❖ *Frequency distributions*

The **Frequency distributions** submenu, under Statistics, then Summaries, provides simple counts *only for the factor variables.*

❖ *Count missing observations*

The **Count missing observations** submenu, under Statistics, then Summaries, does exactly what it says. It gives you a count of missing observations (NAs) for each variable. It's unusual in that it has no options or choices. Click on it, and it proceeds immediately to print out.

❖ Table of statistics

The **Table of statistics** submenu is a bit odd. Figure 2.5 shows a screen shot for it. It puts the numeric variables on the right and calls them "response variables." It puts the factor variables on the left. Underneath them it lists some statistics. You can pick only one statistic. You can pick one or more factors and response variables. Let's pick Mean as our statistic, SEX as our factor variable, and both SATM and SATV as our response variables.

Figure 2.5 The **Table of statistics** screen

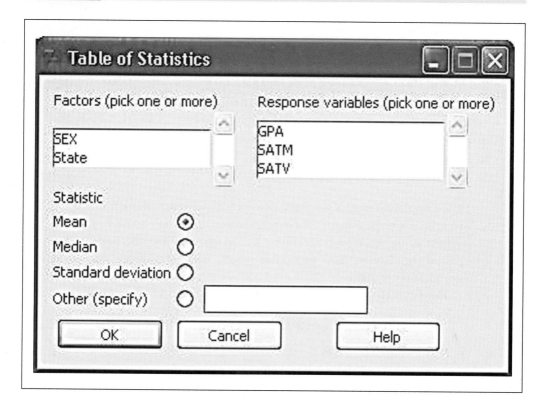

Here's what you get:

> # Table for SATM:

> tapply(SATGPA25R$SATM, list(SEX=SATGPA25R$SEX), mean, na.rm=TRUE)

SEX

   female   male

564.6154   562.0000

> # Table for SATV:

> tapply(SATGPA25R$SATV, list(SEX=SATGPA25R$SEX), mean, na.rm=TRUE)

SEX

   female   male

567.6923   540.0000

You got the mean for SATM separately for females and males and then for SATV. Notice that the command automatically inserted "na.rm=TRUE" (see Section 1–9 if you need a refresher on this point).

❖ *Correlation matrix*

The **Correlation matrix** submenu does exactly what you think it would. It gives you the correlation matrix for whatever variables you choose to include. The default is the Pearson correlation. You could also use the Spearman or do partial correlations. You would not usually encounter partial correlations in introductory statistics.

Here's what you get as output if you pick GPA, SATM, and SATV:

> cor(SATGPA25R[,c("GPA","SATM","SATV")], use="complete.obs")

	GPA	SATM	SATV
GPA	1.0000000	0.2183310	0.2967568
SATM	0.2183310	1.0000000	0.4240854
SATV	0.2967568	0.4240854	1.0000000

❖ Correlation test

The **Correlation test** submenu (see Figure 2.6) performs a statistical test of the null hypothesis (H_0: $\rho = .00$) for the correlation between two variables. You can test only one correlation at a time. The default is a two-sided test. That's what we usually do when testing whether a correlation is "significant," that is, significantly different from zero. However, you can switch to a one-sided test if you wish.

Figure 2.6	The **Correlation test** screen

❖ Shapiro-Wilk test of normality

The final submenu under Statistics, Summaries is the **Shapiro-Wilk test of normality.** As suggested by its title, it tests how well a distribution for a numeric variable fits the theoretical normal distribution. This test is not usually covered in introductory statistics, so we will not describe it in detail.

❖ *The Means Menu: t test and ANOVA*

Remember doing a *t* test in base R? And remember the promise to cover analysis of variance (ANOVA)? Well, now we'll see how to do these in R Commander. Go to Statistics, then Means. Look at the Statistics menu table above to see what's listed under Means. Let's first do a *t* test, testing the hypothesis that there is no difference between males and females in their SATM scores. This is the same *t* test we did in base R. It's an independent-samples *t* test. When you go to Statistics, then Means, then Independent samples t-test, you get Figure 2.7.

Figure 2.7   The **Independent Samples t-Test** screen

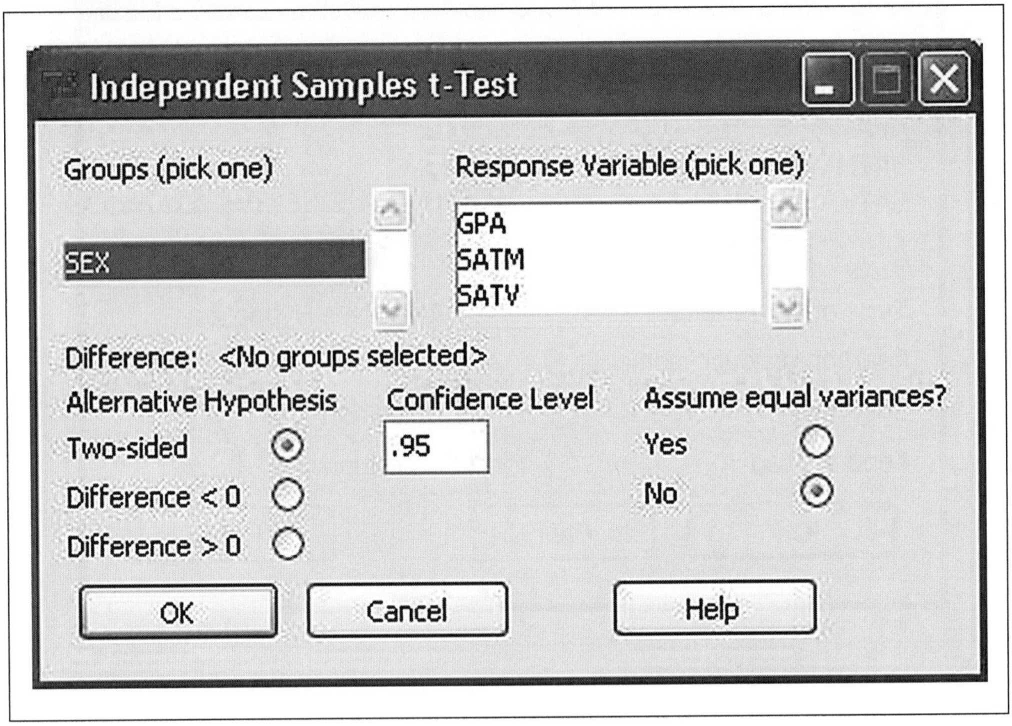

It shows the factor variable for the group contrast and each of the numeric variables. Highlight SATM. Make sure the buttons show "two-sided" and "Yes" for "Assume equal variances?" Let's leave the "confidence level" at its default value of .95. Then, click OK. You get this in your Output Window:

```
> t.test (SATM~SEX, alternative='two.sided', conf.level=.95, var.equal=TRUE,
+   data=SATGPA25R)
```

Two Sample t-test

data: SATM by SEX

t = 0.1001, df = 21, p-value = 0.9212

alternative hypothesis: true difference in means is not equal to 0

95 percent confidence interval:

-51.73848 56.96925

sample estimates:

mean in group female	mean in group male
564.6154	562.0000

You may want to compare this result with what you got when doing the *t* test (SATM~SEX) in base R. You may also want to try some variations on the *t* test you just did in R Commander—for example, changing to "No" for assuming equal variances or changing the confidence interval.

Now, let's do a one-way ANOVA. Go to Statistics, then Means, then One-way ANOVA. You get the screen shown in Figure 2.8.

Figure 2.8 The **One-Way ANOVA** screen

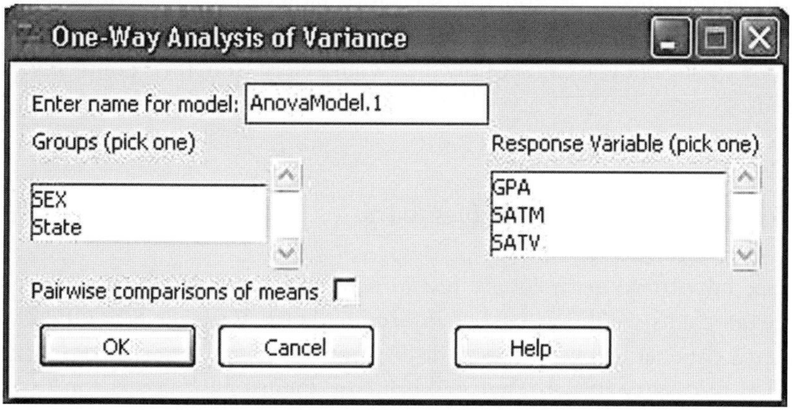

Let's pick State as our Group variable and GPA as the Response variable. Highlight each of those, then click OK. You get this output:

> **AnovaModel.1 <- aov(GPA ~ State, data=SATGPA25R)**

> **summary(AnovaModel.1)**

	Df	Sum Sq	Mean Sq	F value	Pr(>F)
State	2	0.40168	0.20084	1.5783	0.231
Residuals	20	2.54507	0.12725		

2 observations deleted due to missingness

> **numSummary(SATGPA25R$GPA , groups=SATGPA25R$State, statistics=c("mean",**

+   "sd"))

	mean	sd	n
PA	2.922500	0.4007521	12
NY	3.135714	0.3085373	7
NJ	3.247500	0.2628529	4

That is, you get the traditional ANOVA summary table. And it automatically prints out a summary of means, standard deviations, and *n* counts. Notice that, technically, what it did is to automatically call on the "numSummary" function, which we covered in base R.

The Means menu, as you can see, also allows you to do other types of hypothesis tests (e.g., paired *t* test, multiway ANOVA). We will not try to cover these other tests, but you can see how they would work from the examples we have covered.

❖ *Contingency tables and chi-square*

Let's see how to do a chi-square test in R Commander. We'll use exactly the same example as we did in base R in Section 1–10. With the **SATGPA25R** as the active data set, click on the Statistics button, then Contingency tables, and then Two-way table. That will bring up Figure 2.9.

Figure 2.9 The **Contingency Tables Two-Way Table** screen

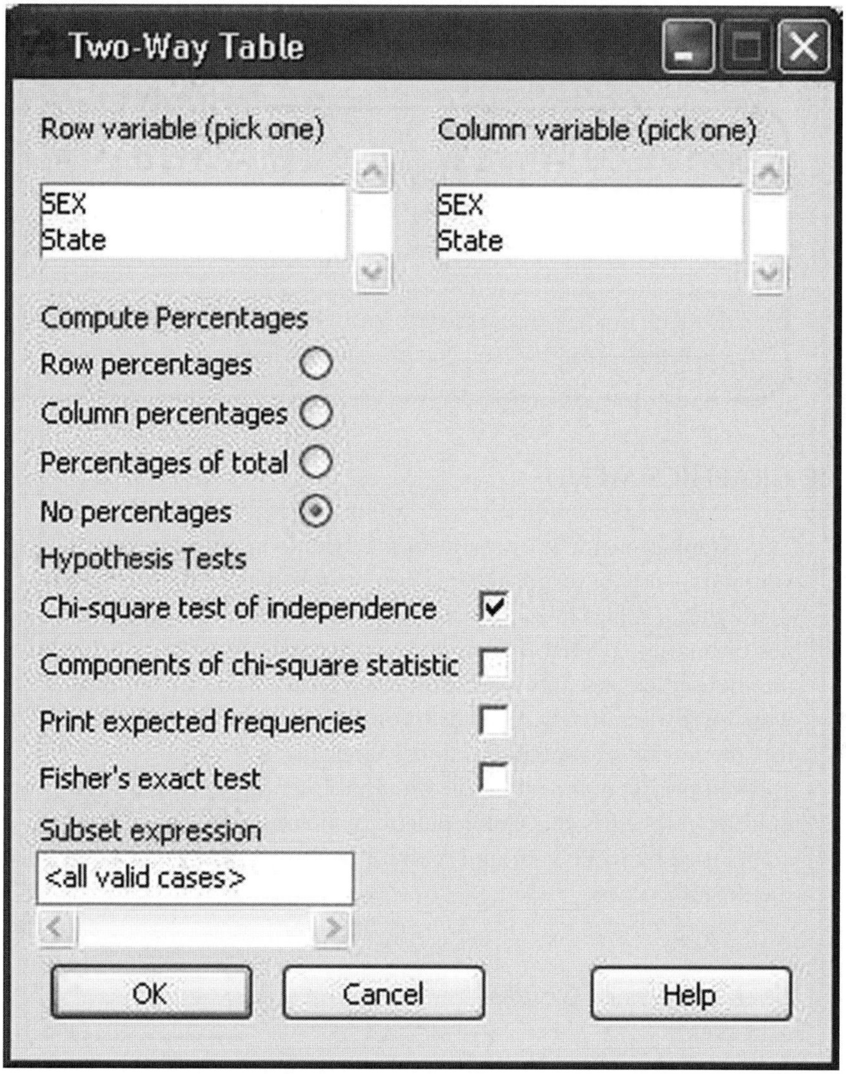

As we did in Section 1–10, make SEX the row variable and State the column variable. Leave all the defaults alone. Click OK.

Notice this about the output. First, it automatically prepares the two-way table for you, even though you didn't request it: Very nice. Second, the actual chi-square output is exactly the same as what we got when we did chisq.test in base R, except that the "warning" appears differently.

✓ **Self-Check 2–4**

Use the **MyData** file created in Self-Check 2–3. If necessary, go to Data, Active data set, Select active data set, highlight it, and click OK.

Then, go to Statistics, Summaries, Numerical summaries, and run the summaries for Age and TestScore.

Next, go to Statistics, Means, Independent samples t-test, and test the hypothesis that boys and girls are equal in TestScore.

2–5 THE GRAPHICS MENU

The **Graphics** menu allows you to prepare a variety of graphical displays for your data—no big surprise there. You obviously need to have an active data set to use the Graphics menu. Entries in the Graphics menu contain a lot of options not ordinarily covered in introductory statistics. We'll pick a few of the commonly used entries and show how they work. Most of the rest of the entries work pretty intuitively, provided you know what the terms mean. Table 2.5 lists the menus and submenus under Graphs.

The opening entry under the Graphics menu, oddly, does not produce any kind of graph. It's the **Color palette,** which allows you to fool around with colors used by R. Play around with it if you want, but we're going to stay with the default colors.

❖ *Examples of Graphs*

Let's do four examples of graphs: pie chart, histogram, boxplot, and scatterplot. Remember to have an active data set open to use these. We'll use the **SATGPA25R** file. Recall that it has three numeric variables (GPA, SATM, and SATV) and two factor variables (SEX and State).

To do a pie chart for the State variable, click on Graphs, scroll to Pie chart, click on it, then highlight State, and click OK. The pie chart will

| Table 2.5 | Master List of Menus and Submenus Under Graphs in R Commander |

Color palette
Index plot
Histogram
Stem-and-leaf display
Boxplot
Quantile comparison plot
Scatterplot
Scatterplot matrix
Line graph
XY conditioning plot
Plot of means
Strip chart
Bar graph
Pie chart

3D graphs	3D scatterplot Identify observations with mouse Save graph to file
Save graph to file	As bitmap As PDF/Postscript/EPS 3D RGL graph

appear in your R Graphics window, which you need to find and maximize to see the chart.

Let's create a histogram for the SATM variable. Click on Graphs, scroll to Histogram, click on it, then highlight SATM, and click OK. The histogram will appear in your R Graphics window.

Let's do a boxplot, comparing males and females on the SATM variable. Click on Graphs, scroll to Boxplot, click on it (see Figure 2.10), then highlight SATM, then click on Plot by groups, and highlight SEX. Now, click OK in this window and in the next window. The boxplots will appear in your R Graphics window.

Figure 2.10 The **Boxplot** screen

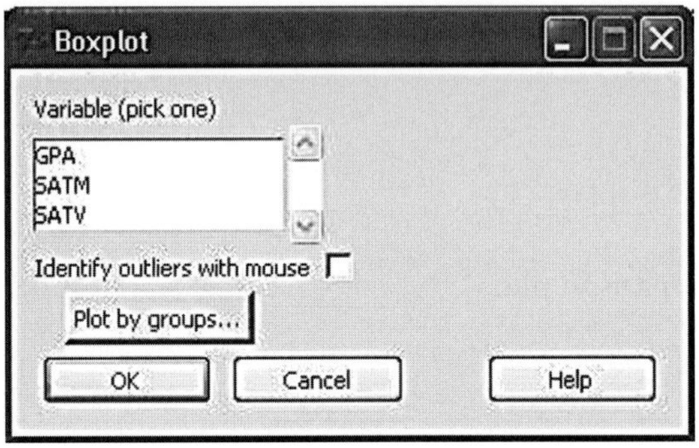

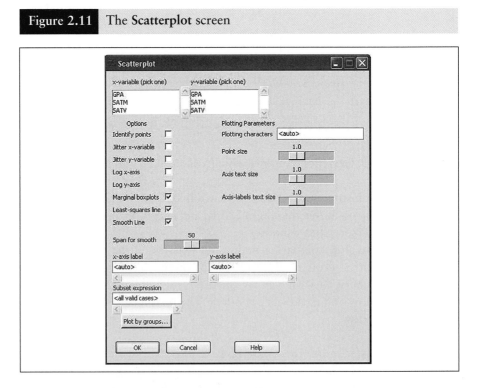

Finally, let's do a scatterplot. Click on Graphs, scroll to Scatterplot, click on it (see Figure 2.11), then highlight one *x* variable and one *y* variable (let's use SATV for *x* and GPA for *y*). Notice that the window contains many options and plotting parameters. We'll leave these alone. Just click OK. The scatterplot will appear in your R Graphics window.

Figure 2.11 The **Scatterplot** screen

You may want to try a few other graphs. As suggested earlier, most of the plots are pretty intuitive, if you know what they are supposed to do.

❖ Changing a Graph's Appearance

R uses certain "default" values when preparing graphs. The Script Window and the Output Window will show what defaults R used. The defaults generally give pretty reasonable graphs. However, you can change these if you want, but it's not that simple. R has a million commands for changing the appearance of graphs. We covered a few of these earlier in base R (Section 1–13). They'll work in R Commander. You just need to add them to the commands that show up in the Script Window, copy and paste the new command right back into the Script Window, and then hit Submit.

Let's try this example. With the **SATGPA25R** file as the active data set in R Commander, click Graphs, then Histogram; select GPA, and click OK. Both the Script Window and Output Window show this:

```
Hist(SATGPA25R$GPA, scale="frequency," breaks="Sturges,"
col="darkgray")
```

Now, in the Script Window, copy that line, and paste it into the next line of the same Script Window. Now, in that line you just pasted, make these changes:

```
Hist(SATGPA25R$GPA, scale="frequency," breaks=4, col=
"black," lwd=3)
```

Now click on Submit. You'll have a new histogram. You changed the number of stacks (also known as bins) from the default "Sturges" (which is a method for determining how many stacks to use). You changed the color (col) from dark gray to black. And you changed the line width (lwd) for the axes. As with graphs prepared in base R, there are tons of ways to change the appearance of graphs in R Commander. We've given just a few illustrations of these here. For our introductory work, we're staying with the defaults. Notice, however, that R Commander allows you to make some changes to the defaults right in the window you use to create a graph. For example, look at the window for Scatterplot. You can change the plotting characters (remember *pch* in Section 1–13), axis text size, and so on right in the window. You might want to try a few of these changes just to get the experience.

Use the **MyData** file created in Self-Check 2–3. If necessary, go to Data, Active data set, Select active data set, highlight it, and click OK.

Then, go to Graphs, Scatterplot (under Options, leave only Least-squares line checked), and run the scatterplot for Age and TestScore.

2–6 THE DISTRIBUTIONS MENU: TWO QUICK EXAMPLES

We said earlier that we'd not cover the **Distributions** menu, with one small exception. Here comes that exception. Remember all those tables at the back of your statistics textbook: the normal distribution, the *t* distribution, chi-square, and so on. Well, you don't need to consult those tables any longer. They're all built into R Commander under the Distributions menu. Let's go to it and present two examples of its use.

For sure, in your statistics course you had to do a problem like this, using a table in the back of the book. In the theoretical normal distribution with a mean of 0 and standard deviation of 1, what percentage of the cases are below a value of –1.5? Here's how to answer that with R Commander.

Go to Distributions, then Continuous distributions, then Normal distribution, then Normal probabilities. You should be looking at Figure 2.12 on your screen.

Figure 2.12   Screen for getting probability for a *z* value

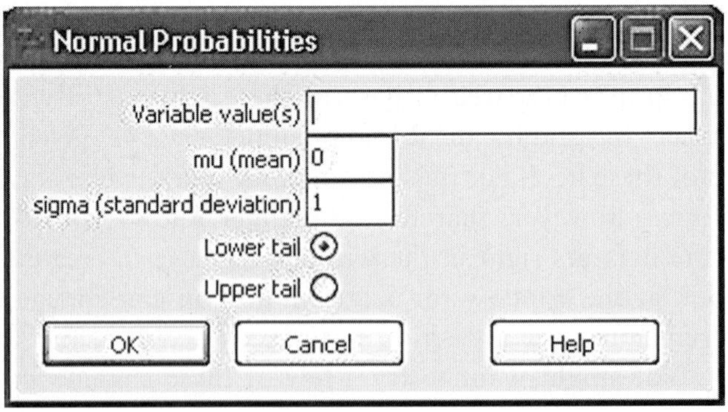

Enter –1.5 for Variable value(s), and click OK. Your Output Window gives this:

```
>pnorm(c(-1.5), mean=0, sd=1, lower.tail=TRUE)

[1] 0.0668072
```

That is, rounding the result, 7% of the cases in the standard normal distribution lie below a value of –1.5. You can change the mean and standard deviation and upper or lower tail as you wish.

Let's do one other example. Recall doing a *t* test and then looking up (in the back of the book) the probability of getting that *t* by chance. Here's how to do it in R Commander. Suppose you got a *t* value of 1.71 with 28 degrees of freedom (*df*). Go to Distributions, then Continuous distributions, then t distribution, then t probabilities. You should be looking at Figure 2.13 on your screen.

Figure 2.13   Screen for getting *p* value for a given *t* value

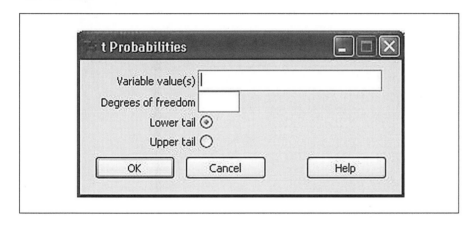

Enter your 1.71 for Variable value(s) and 28 for Degrees of freedom. Your Output Window gives this:

```
>pt(c(1.71), df=28, lower.tail=TRUE)
[1] 0.9508365
```

That is, rounding the result, about 95% of the area in the *t* distribution for *df* = 28 lies below *t* = 1.71 and about 5% above that point. For a two-tailed test, this would give you *p* = .10. No need to look up anything in a table.

After these brief examples of the Distributions menu, you should be able to see how other parts of that menu work. By the way, if you do the whole *t* test in base R or R Commander, the *p* value as well as the *t* value will automatically print out.

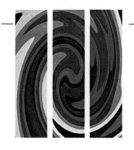

Chapter 3: Some Other Stuff

3-1 A FEW OTHER WAYS TO ENTER DATA

R has a plethora of ways to read data. In fact, it has an entire manual just on this topic (see Section 3–6). We introduced a few of the methods earlier. Here, for the especially ambitious, we'll add two more ways.

❖ *From Word*

First, perhaps somewhat surprisingly, you can create a data set in Microsoft Word (or just about any other word processing system) and read it into R. There are just a few simple rules for doing so. Let's have these three variables for five cases. The variables are Age, Pop (a popularity rating on a 1–9 scale), and Looks (a good-looking rating on a 1–99 scale). Here are the data:

Age	Pop	Looks
18	5	65
20	1	13
21	6	34
NA	9	60
21	7	98

Open a new Word document page. When entering the data, follow these rules:

1. Leave at least one space between each entry, for both variable names and data entries. You can leave additional spaces if you want. Do *not* use tabs.

2. Enter NA for any missing data. Do not just leave a blank.

3. Save the file as a Plain Text file. Let's call it APL, saved as a .txt file in the R folder on the E drive, so the path is E:/R/APL.txt.

4. Access it with read.table, calling it APL, like this:

```
>APL=read.table("E:/R/APL.txt", header=T)
```

You can give the file a different name when you read it into R, if you want. For practice, again try these:

```
>APL

>mean(APL)

>mean(Pop)
```

The latter won't work, remember, until you do this:

```
>attach(APL)
```

Then, again try this:

```
>mean(Pop)
```

And, with all these, remember that file names and variable names are case sensitive. And you don't want any embedded blanks in file names.

❖ *From SPSS*

You may already have a file created in SPSS. You can read it directly into R. Here's how it is done:

1. Make sure you have the package called *foreign* in your R library. It usually downloads automatically with base R. To check, do this:

```
>library( )
```

The *foreign* package should show up. If not, download it using the procedures we described earlier. Then, do this to activate it:

```
>library(foreign)
```

2. Find the exact path to the SPSS file you want to read into R. For example, if you have an SPSS data file called FinalData.sav on your E drive in a folder called Project, the path is: E:/Project/FinalData.sav. Now do this, calling the file FinalR:

```
>FinalR=read.spss('E:/Project/FinalData.sav',to.
data.frame=T)
```

Notice that we have introduced two new items here. The first is read .spss. Make sure you keep spss in lower case. The second is to.data.frame. We used data.frame earlier, but here we use to.data.frame and follow it with the now familiar "= T" where as usual T stands for TRUE. As earlier, be sure to get the exact path name in quotation marks (either single or double). Notice that you don't have to use header "= T" when reading an SPSS file.

After completing the above command, do this:

```
>library( )
```

and your data file will show up.

Or do this:

```
>FinalR
```

and your data file will print out. You can now use R functions on it. Remember to attach the file to access individual variables.

R's *foreign* library has similar commands to read a wide variety of file formats. No doubt you will use some of them as you gain more experience with R.

✓Self-Check 3-1

Assuming you have access to SPSS, bring it up, and create a small data set, say with five cases and two variables. Save it as an SPSS.sav file; name it **MySPSS.sav.** Then, use the procedures just described to bring it up as an R file, calling it **MySPSSinR.** Type MySPSSinR at the R prompt to make sure you have it.

3–2 EXPORTING R RESULTS

For most of the work you do in elementary statistics, whether in base R or R Commander, you'll be content to get the results printed out in the R Console or R Commander Output Window. However, for more advanced work, you may want to save the results in a different format. Of course, you can also copy and paste what you got on the R Console into, say, a Word document. But the output on the R Console usually has a horrible, ugly format, so the procedure is not very helpful, although it is sometimes adequate. See the Helpful Tip on the next page for copy-and-paste procedures. Fortunately, R has ways to output your results to other formats. We call this "exporting" your results.

❖ *Exporting Statistical Summaries From Base R*

Just as R has a million ways to read data in, it has a million ways to read data out, that is, export it. Here, we will introduce just one way to export your results, namely, to an Excel spreadsheet. Once you have your results in an Excel spreadsheet, it's pretty easy to manipulate the format. The procedure will look a bit like what we did in Section 1–7: Reading in Larger Data Sets.

Let's use the SATGPA20R file. We developed this in Section 1–7. You should have it in your R workspace. Check for it with:

```
>ls( )
```

If you don't have it, you can use any other data set you have in your R workspace—just use the name of it appropriately in the following commands.

Let's say we get the *means* for each of the SATGPA20R numeric variables, like this:

```
>mean(SATGPA20R)
```

Now, we'll define a new "R object" called MYMEANS, like this:

```
>MYMEANS=mean (SATGPA20R)
```

R creates a thing called MYMEANS. We now write it to an Excel-readable file, telling R where to put it. We'll put it on the E drive in folder R and call the new file MYMEANS, which will be a *.csv file*, so the exact path is E:/R/MYMEANS.csv. (.csv stands for comma-separated values.) So do this:

```
>write.csv(MYMEANS, file="E:/R/MYMEANS.csv")
```

HT   Helpful Tip

Special Note for Copy and Paste

If you copy and paste output from the R Console to another document—for example, a Word document—use a monospaced font (e.g., Arial monospaced) in the new document. This will give you much better spacing of the output.

For the output you see on page 44 in this book, here's what you get if you copy and paste the output in the commonly used Times New Roman font:

```
> summary(SATGPA25R)
   SEX     State     SATV          SATM          GPA
female:14  PA :12  Min.   :390.0  Min.   :430.0  Min.   :2.380
male :11   NY : 7  1st Qu.:495.0  1st Qu.:525.0  1st Qu.:2.870
           NJ : 4  Median :560.0  Median :560.0  Median :3.030
           NA's: 2  Mean   :555.7  Mean   :563.5  Mean   :3.046
                   3rd Qu.:620.0  3rd Qu.:595.0  3rd Qu.:3.210
                   Max.   :670.0  Max.   :720.0  Max.   :3.730
                   NA's   : 2.0  NA's   : 2.0
```

Very hard to read!

Here is the same output in Arial monospaced font:

```
> summary(SATGPA25R)
   SEX        State       SATV          SATM          GPA
female:14   PA  :12    Min.   :390.0  Min.   :430.0  Min.   :2.380
male  :11   NY  : 7    1st Qu.:495.0  1st Qu.:525.0  1st Qu.:2.870
            NJ  : 4    Median:560.0   Median:560.0   Median:3.030
            NA's : 2   Mean  :555.7   Mean  :563.5   Mean  :3.046
                       3rd Qu. 620.0  3rd Qu.:595.0  3rd Qu.:3.210
                       Max.   :670.0  Max.   :720.0  Max.   :3.730
                       NA's   :  2.0  NA's     :2.0
```

See how nicely everything lines up.

A monospaced font will use more space than a non-monospaced font, so you may need to reduce the font size to have the output fit conveniently in your document.

This reads the MYMEANS "thing" (an R object) into MYMEANS (as a .csv file) on the E drive. Once MYMEANS is there, you can read it as an Excel file. Just open Excel, find MYMEANS, and read it.

Let's do another one. Let's put the correlation matrix for the numeric variables in SATGPA20R into an Excel-readable file called SATCOR.csv in the R folder on the E drive. Do this:

```
>SATCOR=cor(SATGPA20R)
```

Then:

```
>write.csv(SATCOR, file="E:/R/SATCOR.csv")
```

Now go find SATCOR.csv on your E drive, and open it with Excel.

If you want to check that you have SATCOR.csv in the R Console, do this:

```
>read.csv("SATCOR.csv")
```

To repeat, R has numerous ways to export data. We have illustrated just one very helpful way to do so.

❖ *Exporting Graphs From Base R*

Exporting graphs from base R is simple. With a graph showing in the R Graphics window, just right click on it, "Copy as metafile" or "Save as metafile," and put it where you want it, that is, directly into another document or into a saved file.

✓**Self-Check 3–2**

Open a blank page in Word. In the R Console, do the plot of the RS and MS variables we created in Section 1–13; that is, plot (RS, MS). You probably still have these variables in your R workspace; if not, create them. With the plot showing, put your cursor anywhere on the plot, and right click. Then, left click on "Copy as metafile." Now, go to your Word document, right click, then left click on Paste. Your plot will appear in the Word document. You can "size it" to fit your needs.

❖ *Exporting Results From R Commander*

Exporting results from R Commander is also easy. It's much like saving something in Word or Excel. For statistical summaries, after running a summary (e.g., Numerical Summaries), go to the File menu, click "Save output as," give the file a name and destination, and click Save. Notice that the file will be saved as a text (.txt) file.

To save a graph prepared from R Commander, follow exactly the same steps as outlined above for saving a graph from base R. Notice that R Commander puts a graph in the R Graphics window, not on the R Commander Output Window.

3–3 BONUS: BUILD YOUR OWN FUNCTIONS

Do this section only if you're feeling pretty confident and inventive. Otherwise, skip it. No other material in the book depends on doing this section.

So far, we've done a lot with R functions. Guess what—you can build your own functions and save them in your workspace just as you have stored data files. You give the function a name. Just don't use a name already reserved in R. When building your own function, you can use existing R functions as well as simple arithmetic operations. Let's say you want to build a function that yields the mean of a variable plus two times its standard deviation. This is a very weird statistic—I can't imagine why you'd want it—so we'll name it "weirdstat."

Here's how to proceed:

```
>weirdstat=function(x) mean(x)+(2*sd(x))
```

This says we're defining weirdstat as a function for a variable, as indicated by *function(x)*. This is followed by the definition of the function, in this case the mean of *x* plus two times the standard deviation of *x*. When we use the function weirdstat, we'll replace *x* with the name of a variable.

Let's do it. Enter in the R Console:

```
>weirdstat=function(x) mean(x)+(2*sd(x))
```

Then, enter this (assuming you have the SATGPA20R file active):

```
>weirdstat(GPA)
```

You get this:

```
[1] 3.912333
```

which is the mean of GPA plus two times its standard deviation—a very weird statistic.

R will save your newly defined function in your R workspace, just as it saves a data set, when you click "Yes" on exiting R. You can show that R saved your function with the ls ( ) command. You can remove the function with the rm (file) command. See Section 1–12 for a review of these commands.

✓ Self-Check 3–3

Suppose you want to define your own function, call it **MYSTAT,** that will calculate the difference between the mean and the median for a variable. Use the procedures just described to define this new function. Then, apply it to any small data set you have in your workspace. To verify that it worked, use the mean and median functions separately to show that **MYSTAT** gives the correct result.

3–4 AN EXAMPLE OF AN ADD-ON PACKAGE

This section is not crucial for introductory statistics students. Nothing in the other sections depends on it. However, you hear so much about R "add-on" packages that you might find it useful to take the 15 minutes to work through this material.

All the functions we have used thus far are a part of *base R* and the *stats* package or *graphics* package that downloads automatically with base R. As noted in our list of R advantages, the R network also includes many add-on packages. Each package has some specialized purposes and the routines to deal with those purposes. There are many such add-on packages, with more becoming available all the time. We'll work through the steps of adding one such package and describe how to start using it.

❖ Getting Information About Packages

First, we need to describe how to get information about the packages. To get a list of packages, follow these steps:

1. Go to http://cran.r-project.org/. That's where you might have obtained base R to start with.

2. On the left-hand side, just under CRAN, click on Task Views.

3. This will give you a list of *categories* of add-on packages—not the packages themselves. At the time of writing this, there are 23 categories, starting with Bayesian and going on to Time Series.

4. To get a list of the actual packages, click on the link for a category.

5. After clicking on a category, the actual packages appear as highlighted links. Each has a very brief description. The descriptions tend to be highly cryptic and specialized. Many packages have obscure names.

6. To find out what's really in a package, click on the highlighted link for that package.

7. Before proceeding with the next step, let's go to the Psychometrics category. Click on it. You'll see a host of links to specific packages, each briefly described.

8. When you find a package that looks like it might be useful, *do not* immediately download it. First, click on the package name. Now, you get a more specific description of it but still pretty brief and quite technical. Do it now for the *psychometric* package. Note that *psychometric* is a package under the Psychometrics category—a little confusing.

9. The key thing now is to go to the Reference manual, always available in pdf format. You want to bring this up, check it out, see if it's comprehensible (some manuals make sense only to very experienced programmers), and see if the package will do what you want it to do.

10. Bring up the Reference manual for the *psychometric* package. It will have a table of contents on the left-hand side and a copy of the first page on the right-hand side. You'll probably need to adjust the viewing size in order to read it. The first page contains basic descriptive information, such as author, date created, and so on.

11. Scrolling down in the Reference manual, we find out what "packages" are all about. They are really collections of more "functions"—remember those from earlier, such as mean, sd, plot, and cor—which the package authors have created to deal with special issues not already covered in base R. Some packages also contain data sets used as examples in the package.

❖ *Installing an Add-On Package*

Now we are ready to install a package and use some of its functions. We are going to install the *psychometric* package. This is one of the packages listed in several categories in CRAN. We'll follow the steps used earlier to load the R Commander package (see Section 2–1).

To summarize, at the top of the R Console, click Packages, then Install package(s). In the next screen, scroll to your favorite CRAN Mirror site, highlight it, and click OK. In the next window, scroll to *psychometric*, highlight it, and click OK.

Remember that you need an Internet connection to load a new package. Once it is loaded onto your computer, you don't need the Internet connection to use the package.

To make sure you have the *psychometric* package in your library, do this:

```
>library( )
```

and check to see that *psychometric* is there. Then to activate it, do this:

```
>library(psychometric)
```

❖ Using an Add-On Package

As noted above, an add-on package is a collection of specially written functions. We will now illustrate just a few of these from the *psychometric* package.

Recall that we examined the Reference manual for the *psychometric* package earlier. We looked at some of its functions. Now that we have the package loaded into our library, we can access the list of functions like this:

```
>help(psychometric)
```

Do it. Then, scroll to r.nil (also listed as r.null). This function tests the hypothesis that the correlation in the population is zero (i.e., $\rho = .00$). Notice how the function is defined (under Usage):

```
r.nil(r, n)
```

r.nil is the function. Recall from Section 1–8 that the entries in parentheses are called "arguments"—not a very helpful term. They are what you need to enter to get the function to work. That is, the function will operate on these entries, the arguments.

For the r.nil function, all we need is r (the correlation coefficient) and n (the number of cases on which r is based). Let's say we have $r = .40$, based on 50 cases. Do this in the R Console:

```
>r.nil(.40, 50)
```

Here's what you get back:

H0.rNot0		t	df	p
1	0.4	3.023716	48	0.002000336

You have a line showing that you are testing the hypothesis that r is not equal to 0 (H0.rNot0), followed by headings for the t test value (t), degrees of freedom (df), and the probability (p) of getting an r as great as .40 if ρ really is 0 in the population. On the next line, you get our familiar line number (1), followed by r (0.4), t (3.023716), df (48), and p (0.002000336). For reporting purposes, we would usually round the t and p to two or three decimal places. In any case, using the conventional alpha levels for hypothesis tests, we would reject the hypothesis that ρ = .00 at the .01 level (i.e., $p < .01$).

Let's try one more function. Let's test the hypothesis that the correlations are equal in two groups. For example, we know that SAT Math scores have a moderate correlation with GPA. But is the degree of correlation the same for males and females? We start with a version of the null hypothesis that says the correlation is the same (no difference) for males and females. We take samples of 50 males and 50 females, calculate correlations between SAT Math and GPA for the two groups, and get r for males =.35 and r for females = .30. Should we reject the null hypothesis? Is that a significant difference? In the *psychometric* package, we use the rdif.nul function. Find it, using this:

```
>help(psychometric)
```

Under Usage, it shows

```
rdif.nul(r1, r2, n1, n2)
```

So we need the two correlations (r1 = r for males, r2 = r for females) and the two sample sizes, 50 males and 50 females, so we will enter this in the R Console:

```
>rdif.nul(.35, .30, 50, 50)
```

It returns the following:

zDIF   **p**

1 0.2711024 0.3931561

The appropriate statistical test is a z test for a difference between two correlations. The top line gives the z value (zDIF) and labels the corresponding p value, that is, the probability that you would get a difference as large as we got if, in fact, the null hypothesis is true. On the next line, we get our familiar line number (1), then the z test value (0.2711024), and then the p value (0.3931561). The p value is well above .05, so we retain the null hypothesis.

As you can see by entering >help(psychometric), the package has many other functions. Our two examples illustrate how to use a package. Two warnings about the packages. First, the output—and this is generally true of R—is not very elegant. Second, descriptions of some functions (under Usage) and their "arguments" require very specialized knowledge.

3–5 KEEPING UP-TO-DATE

R and its various add-on packages change from time to time. The main R home page will alert you to changes in base R. Check the version number. This book used R version 2.9.0, released on April 17, 2009, for base R and Version 1.4–10 for R Commander. Authors of add-on packages may change them any time. You simply need to be alert to such changes. When you see that a new version has been released, simply download it using the procedures we described earlier for downloading.

Successive versions of R tend to work seamlessly for the simple kinds of procedures we have used in this book. Notes on changes always accompany new releases. You can find these on the R home page (http://cran-r.project.org). When navigating around R's home page, you'll notice that it exists in an exceptionally dynamic environment: lots of exchanges between users, new wrinkles in this or that part of R, helpful links to other sources, and so on.

3–6 GOING FURTHER: SELECTED REFERENCES

We've provided a bare-bones introduction to R. There's a whole lot we haven't covered. With this introduction, you should be ready to go further with other resources. Here are some of the resources that may help you. Use the first two entries for R manuals, documentation, and so on.

- Following is the home page for R: http://www.r-project.org/
- Download R from http://cran.r-project.org/
- Go to this URL for a host of supplementary introductions to R: http://cran .r-project.org/other-docs.html

Here are some books that may be useful:

- Dalgaard, P. (2008). *Introductory statistics with R* (2nd ed.). New York: Springer. Covers an introduction to R with a fulsome range of statistical procedures (363 pages).

- Everitt, B. S., & Hothorn, T. (2006). *A handbook of statistical analyses using R*. Boca Raton, FL: Chapman & Hall.

  This book gives many examples of statistical analyses in R. Associated data sets are available in R add-on packages. Quite technical—not for the faint-hearted (275 pages).

- Fox, J. (2005). *Getting started with the R Commander*.

  This is the manual accessed through the Help menu in R Commander. It is a 22-page pdf file.

- Murrell, P. (2005). *R graphics*. Boca Raton, FL: Chapman & Hall.

  This is a useful supplement to Chapter 12: "Graphical Procedures" in the official R manual (Venables et al., 2009—see below). Parts of this book are available online at http://www.stat.auckland.ac.nz/~paul/RGraphics/rgraphics.html

- R Development Core Team. (2009). R Data Import/Export version 2.9.0.

  This is the official manual on importing and exporting files from R, available in pdf format at the cran.r site under Documentation, Manuals. Available at http://cran.r-project.org/

- Venables, W. N., Smith, D. M., & the R Development Core Team. (2009). An introduction to R. Notes on R: A programming environment for data analysis and graphics version 2.9.0.

  This is the "official" introduction to R, available in pdf format at the cran.r site under Documentation, Manuals. Available at http://cran.r-project.org/

- Verzani, J. (n.d.). *SimpleR: Using R for introductory statistics*.

  This textbook on R (114 pages) is available online at http://cran.r-project.org/doc/contrib/Verzani-SimpleR.pdf

To cite the use of R for statistical work, R documentation recommends the following:

R Development Core Team. (2009). *R: A language and environment for statistical computing. R Foundation for Statistical Computing,* Vienna, Austria. ISBN 3–900051–07–0, URL http://www.R-project.org

The recommended citation to the use of R may change from time to time. To get the latest citation, type "citation ( )" at the > prompt in the R Console.

Handy List of a Few Crucial Commands in Base R

In this list, for **file**, insert the name of a data file; for **function**, insert the name of a function; for **variable**, insert the name of a variable you have in R; and for **package**, insert the name of an R package. This list contains only one example (mean) of the many functions in the R "stats" package. For other commonly used statistical functions, see the table on page 23. Where nothing appears in parentheses, such as this ( ), put nothing in! The "Details" column shows the page numbers where this book first introduces the command.

R Command	What It Does	Details
>**variable**	Lists values of the named variable	8
>**file**	Lists values of the entire named data file	15
>quit ( )	To exit R	10
>mean (**variable**)	Calculates the mean of the variable	11
>mean (**file**)	Calculates means of all variables in file	15
>**file** = read.table ("exact path," . . .)	Reads a .txt file containing data. For . . . add header = T (or F)	14
>**file**.choose ( )	Helps find the exact path to a file in the computer	15
>attach (**file**)	Unpacks a data set to operate on individual variables	16
>**file** = data.frame (**variable, variable,** . . .)	Puts two or more existing variables into a single data set	16
>help (**function**)	Gets R's help menu for a function	17
>example (**function**)	Gets R's example(s) for a function	18
>**function** (**file**, na.rm = T)	For a function, operates on a file or variable, to remove missing data	19
>ls ( )	Lists currently active files, variables, and custom functions in your R workspace	24
>rm (**file or variable**)	Removes a file, variable, or custom function from your R workspace	25
>library (**package**)	Activates an R package already downloaded	32
>library ( )	Lists packages currently active in your library	33

Index

Note: Special Symbols: <-, 9 #. *See* Notation symbol

Supporting researchers for more than 40 years

Research methods have always been at the core of SAGE's publishing program. Founder Sara Miller McCune published SAGE's first methods book, *Public Policy Evaluation*, in 1970. Soon after, she launched the *Quantitative Applications in the Social Sciences* series—affectionately known as the "little green books."

Always at the forefront of developing and supporting new approaches in methods, SAGE published early groundbreaking texts and journals in the fields of qualitative methods and evaluation.

Today, more than 40 years and two million little green books later, SAGE continues to push the boundaries with a growing list of more than 1,200 research methods books, journals, and reference works across the social, behavioral, and health sciences. Its imprints—Pine Forge Press, home of innovative textbooks in sociology, and Corwin, publisher of PreK–12 resources for teachers and administrators—broaden SAGE's range of offerings in methods. SAGE further extended its impact in 2008 when it acquired CQ Press and its best-selling and highly respected political science research methods list.

From qualitative, quantitative, and mixed methods to evaluation, SAGE is the essential resource for academics and practitioners looking for the latest methods by leading scholars.

For more information, visit **www.sagepub.com**.